T0286008

THE DEATH OF LIBERTY©

THE SOCIALIST DESTRUCTION OF AMERICA'S FREEDOMS USING THE INCOME TAX

DAVID THOMAS ROBERTS

The Death of Liberty©

ISBN-13: 978-1-948035-12-5

Published by Defiance Press & Publishing, LLC
Printed in the United States of America
10 9 8 7 6 5 4 3 2 1

Defiance Press & Publishing, LLC
info@defiancepress.com

Also available in audiobook format on Amazon©

Proudly Published in the Republic of Texas

ALSO BY DAVID THOMAS ROBERTS

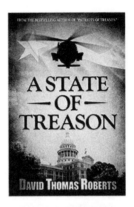

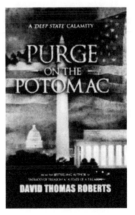

To my wife, Rose, who was an author's widow on most nights and weekends for months as I researched and worked on this book. Her eternal patience and grace allowed me to chase my dream of telling this untold story to America.

"Here, in the United States, we are alarmed by new calls to adopt socialism in our country. America was founded on liberty and independence — not government coercion, domination, and control. We are born free, and we will stay free. Tonight, we renew our resolve that America will never be a socialist country."

—Donald J. Trump
45th President of the United States
State of the Union Address
February 4, 2019

CONTENTS

Foreword by Robert G. Bernhoft, Esq.

1 Have We Lost Our Sense of Liberty? 1

2 Progressivism & the Roots of American Class Warfare 11

3 Teddy Roosevelt: The Progressive's Trojan Horse 19

4 Constitutional Taxes 27

5 The GOP's Grand Mistake 37

6 Pay as You Go—A Direct Assault on Liberty 41

7 The Morality of the Income Tax 53

8 Patriotism & Paying Taxes 79

9 The Benevolent Welfare State via the Income Tax 91

10 Compliance Costs—Paying for Your Loss of Freedoms 99

11 The Progressive's Secret Weapon: Fear 109

12 The Horror Stories 121

13 Punish Thine Enemies 155

14 An Enemy of the State 167

15 The Root of the Problem 175

16 Lipstick on a Pig 179

17 The Flat Tax and the FairTax 185

18 Understanding the Enemy 191

19 Conservative Action Plan 197

References

Index

Robert G. Bernhoft, Esq.

America's #1 Tax Attorney

"Wesley Snipes acquitted of tax fraud."
— The *New York Times*

"Big Victory in [Ralph] Nadar Open Ballot Ruling"
— *Reuters*

"Protestors [Joseph Banister] Win a Case Over IRS"
— The *New York Times*

"Woman [Vernice Kuglin] triumphs over IRS in million-dollar tax case."
— *World Net*

David Thomas Roberts and I first met some time ago when he contacted me to represent him in an IRS audit. Nothing unusual about that: I'd risen to the top of my legal field by successfully defending American citizens in civil and criminal tax controversies for many years. *The IRS auditing a successful entrepreneur?* That was an everyday occurrence in my professional world. After all, when you're looking for money, you go where the money is — a true statement of reality when it comes to the IRS and Congressional tax policy — however cynical — and a foreshadowing of Roberts' blockbuster exposé of the federal income tax's origins in socialism and its pernicious effects on America today.

It quickly became clear, though, that Roberts' case would be anything but business as usual. The IRS had started auditing Roberts on a near-yearly basis for many years. In fact, Roberts may be the most audited man in America. Perhaps, the IRS targeted Roberts for being a founder of the Tea Party movement? Perhaps, he found his way onto one of many "lists" of loyal American oppositionists committed to constitutional government and liberty?

I'd certainly litigated more than my share of IRS misconduct over the years—exposing IRS illegal surveillance, perjury, fabrication of evidence, witness intimidation, and trial misconduct along the way. So, I wasn't particularly surprised that Roberts had garnered the IRS's attention.

Point is: *he* was surprised....

Roberts' deep-rooted Americanism was justifiably jarred, and jarred badly, by the growing realization that the IRS's enforcement of direct taxation on labor was an ugly affront to every cherished principle he held dear. Anathema to fundamental rights and liberties under the Constitution. Anathema to the Fourth Amendment's guarantee of the security and privacy of our persons, houses, papers, and effects. Anathema to the Fifth Amendment's hoary prohibition against being compelled to be a witness against oneself. Thus are the origins of Roberts' compelling new book, *The Death of Liberty*, his second work of nonfiction and fifth book overall.

Roberts quickly disabused my initial concern that he intended to pedal "one more" in a long line of books by other authors attempting to tell us what the income tax really is, as a legal matter.

Supreme Court cases opine over direct and indirect taxation, apportionment, the meaning of the Sixteenth Amendment, and the definition of income. Some argue the modern income tax is a direct tax, lacking apportionment, and, therefore, unconstitutional. Others say the Sixteenth Amendment was not properly ratified; hence, the income tax is a nullity.

Even for an accomplished constitutional scholar and attorney, it's enough to make you go blind. No, Roberts' book would explore and expose the inextricable linkages between American socialism—as a political, economic, and social theory—and the federal income tax from its earliest origins to its pernicious realities today. An accomplished researcher, Roberts starts with touching on the Civil War context, then moves briskly through the late 1800s Industrial

Revolution and the politics behind calls to "tax the rich." Not even Teddy Roosevelt is immune to Roberts' sharp pen.

Roberts lays bare the unvarnished "bipartisan" history of America's move toward the direct federal taxation of labor, which is, as Roberts correctly points out, a plank of *The Communist Manifesto*.

Wisely eschewing endless legal fights over the constitutional and legal aspects of the income tax, Roberts recognizes that in America today, the question of the income tax is a *political* one, not a legal one. Whole industries and their well-oiled lobbyists dine at the Bacchanalian banquet created by a tax code so complex that President Ronald Reagan once admonished: "Our federal tax system is, in short, utterly impossible, utterly unjust and completely unproductive, [it] reeks with injustice and is fundamentally un-American...it has earned rebellion and it's time we rebelled."

As President Reagan so well understood, pharisaical legal screeds are not helpful when dealing with an income tax problem so entrenched that its legal, economic, political, and social prerequisites and demands actually form societal bedrock—not to mention bedrock polluted by socialism's reverence for the collective over the individual and the destructive consequences of that misbegotten system.

Un-American indeed.

Here, Roberts shines. Moving to more current IRS scandals and abuse horror stories, he persuasively connects the income tax's undiscovered socialistic history with the burgeoning loss of fundamental rights in America. Roberts makes a cogent case that IRS abuse is a direct consequence of its origins in socialism, with its inevitable abuses of power and authoritarian control by the few over the many. In Roberts' view, the IRS carries the main spear, if not the totalitarian tip, of socialism's epic fight to destroy our uniquely American rule of law system and the rights and liberties it protects.

Every socialist state is complete when it can wield an apparently legal mechanism against its citizens—at once an information, surveillance, and enforcement bureau that becomes increasingly unaccountable. The man credited as the father of the Soviet Union's infamous KGB, Lavrentiy Beria, would envy the power and capabilities of America's IRS. Yet, many Americans remain ignorant of this important history.

Enter David Thomas Roberts.

Socialism is the disease, the income tax the malignancy, and Roberts' *The Death of Liberty* the cure. Commenced well before American socialism recrudesced in the fresh new faces of the self-described Democratic Socialists of the Democrat Party's "progressive" left wing, Roberts' income tax exposé is eerily prescient.

The Death of Liberty exposes the historic failures of American attempts to address "income inequality" with socialistic wealth redistribution and centralized control through the income tax. Engaging, vibrant, and timely, Roberts provides a modern reader's guide to understanding the unseemly impulses that lie beneath the current calls for economic justice, the siren song of socialism and its many acolytes, and why all of us should do something about it before it's too late.

THE DEATH OF LIBERTY©

1

★

HAVE WE LOST OUR SENSE OF LIBERTY?

"In short, when this (16th) amendment became part of the Constitution, in 1913, the absolute right of property in the United States was violated. That, of course, is the essence of socialism."

—Frank Chodorov (1887–1966)
Author, Publisher, & Conservative Libertarian

Unfortunately, President Trump's statement in his 2019 State of the Union that America will *never* be a socialist country is 106 years too late.

We already are.

And, we only *think* we live in a free country.

Stop kidding yourself. I did a long time ago. We have dishonored the legacy and sacrifices of our Founding Fathers.

The home of the free and the brave?

Certainly, on the battlefield, we have proven to be brave. But, here at home, we have allowed ourselves to be governed and controlled by spineless politicians who have taken a horribly constructed and unconstitutional idea and exploited our rampant societal civic illiteracy and apathetic laziness to advance an ill-conceived progressive ideology, which has robbed us of our God-given liberties, possibly forever.

Does the average American realize — or even care — that they are living under a complete Marxist ideology that has infected and metastasized over the last 106 years to impact almost every facet of their daily lives?

Gone is the rugged self-reliance inherited by our pre-1913-era immigrant shopkeepers, farmers, ranchers, and tradesman—and with it, our American idealism that was so instrumental in our founding and in propelling America to the beacon of freedom it once was. Today, incredibly, more Americans work for federal, state, and local government than own a business.[1]

What would our Founders think of it? How, in the most freedom-loving country in human history, did Americans let it happen and come to accept it as part of their life? Why do Americans put up with it? Do Americans have the fortitude to ever fix it permanently?

As I began writing, those questions kept me up at night. The original intent of this book was to be focused on the abuses of the Internal Revenue Service (IRS), the loss of our Bill of Rights in dealing with tax issues, the weaponization of the IRS, and the recent litany of IRS political targeting scandals. But, the more abuses I uncovered, the more it begged the question: *How did we get so far off track from our Founders original design?*

It's important to note here that this is neither a book on protesting taxes nor one that tells you how *not* to pay income taxes. Is it a conspiracy book? Only in the sense that the Sixteenth Amendment has, in fact, obliterated our Bill of Rights, and because it confirms that the IRS is the darkest and most feared agency in our federal government. The progressive income tax is likely the very definition of—and the original core element of—the *Deep State.* Along with the FBI, the IRS is the tip of the spear for the enforcement of Deep State dogmas—although, it can be argued that the IRS has literally no checks and balances to oversee the abuse. The progressives in both parties have brought us to this point, significantly aided by the literal dumbing-down of the general populace.

The progressive income tax and the ruthless agency that wields its mighty power is more of a threat to our freedom than any foreign enemy, and every year, it grows more ominous for future generations.

Politicians have been drunk on the endless stream of money that flows into Washington, D.C., from the income tax that

2

manipulates the tax code to rewarding government cronies and punishing their political enemies. The progressive income tax is the grandest "social justice" scheme ever invented.

Do I believe taxes are a necessary evil? Of course. There is certainly a role for federal government functions such as the military defense, currency, immigration, and interstate commerce. But, my style of government (and that of the Founders) is more suited to the 1776–1913 style of a governing, specifically limited within the Constitution's enumerated powers.

How could we have let our liberties ebb away? How can we fix it, if we don't understand how it occurred in the first place?

Can you imagine those patriots in the Boston Tea Party allowing a huge, centralized government to take the very *first* fruits of their labor and have access to all their private papers? A simple tax on tea ignited the American Revolution; yet, we are robbed of our income on payday, and we live under a perpetual, unspoken threat that the IRS can seize our papers, bank accounts, businesses, and assets.

Imagine a revenue officer telling Samuel Adams he's being "audited on his labor and income" or Patrick Henry he must "produce all his private receipts and papers" or Thomas Jefferson he can't "invoke the Fifth Amendment on self-incrimination" in a tax case?

The American colonists had no toleration for tax collectors. The colonists' threats to tar and feather tax collectors chased many of those same collectors out of the colonies. The Whiskey Rebellion, arguably caused by large government proponent Alexander Hamilton, was seen as a direct tax on small distillers in favor of larger East Coast distillers and was met by noncompliance, violence, and riots. This tax propelled the anti-tax Jefferson to win the next presidential election and the formation of the Republican Party.[2]

America was staunchly anti-tax at the core of its inception. On the properties of many American homes and farms, you could find liberty poles, an American custom largely forgotten. Erecting a liberty pole indicated you wanted tyranny — and government — out of your life. So, what monumental moment in history changed this for America?

3

Well, the insidious action by politicians in the early 1900s lacked a cataclysmic or decisive moment. And, there wasn't a typical crisis, such as a war, that convinced Congress or the ratifying state legislators to adopt a solution to something where a problem didn't exist. It wasn't that simple.

There are numerous major milestones throughout American history where events or circumstances seriously challenged our young Constitutional Republic and changed the course and direction of the country forever. Certainly, the ratification of the United States Constitution was one of those moments. The Civil War was another, as was ending slavery, World War I, Women's Suffrage, the Federal Reserve Act, the Crash of 1929, the New Deal, *United States v. Butler*, World War II, JFK's assassination, the Civil Rights Act, the Vietnam War, landing on the moon, *Roe v. Wade*, and winning the Cold War, among others.

But, few curriculum history books (if any) discuss the major course redirection of the country that was taken with the ratification of the Sixteenth Amendment, which allowed for the *direct* taxation of American citizens. Congress had already tried a direct income tax in 1894, but it was rightly ruled unconstitutional and was overturned by the U.S. Supreme Court.

At the time of our founding, American colonists were the most literate citizens in the world. They were voracious readers and were enormously interested in civics, citizenship, and how the government operated. At a minimum, they knew what they *didn't* want, based on their experiences with the British crown. They didn't want a monarchy or taxation without representation; they didn't want a direct tax.

Compare that to today. We're at the peak of the Information Age, with an incredible amount of data, history, and references at our fingertips, right there on our smartphones. Yet, I'd wager the average college student couldn't recite what constitutes the three branches of government.

Consider this October 4, 2018 *Wall Street Journal* editorial:

4

Most Americans can't pass the civics test required of immigrants. These days it's popular to lament that immigrants are destroying America's national identity, but maybe we're getting it backward. When the Woodrow Wilson National Fellowship Foundation recently put questions from the U.S. Citizenship Test to the American citizen, only one in three could pass the multiple-choice test.

It's embarrassing. According to the foundation, only 13% of Americans knew when the Constitution was ratified, and 60% didn't know which countries the United States fought in World War II. Most couldn't correctly identify the 13 original colonies, with at least is something of a teaser. But only 24% could identify something that Ben Franklin was famous for, and 37% thought it was for inventing the light bulb.

Even with a highly contested Supreme Court nomination now in play in the Senate, 57% of Americans couldn't say how many Justices are on the Court. Older Americans did much better than younger Americans—only 19% of the under-45 crowd passed—which probably reflects the declining state of American public schools. None of this augurs well for the future of self-government.

We've always thought it important that immigrants must pass a test on the basics of American history and civics before they can be sworn in as citizens. Immigrants who are motivated to become citizens will take the time to learn. The real threat to American freedom is the failure of current citizens to learn even the most basic facts about U.S. history and government.[3]

The visible loss of Liberty doesn't occur in very public and demonstrable tranches to most; instead, we lose our liberties like a slow-moving glacier gobbling up our freedoms incrementally over time. America has had ample opportunity to throw off these encroachments to freedom, but as more time has passed between 1913 and today, fewer and fewer Americans really understand what

Liberty looks like. If you were born after 1913, you have never experienced the complete Liberty enjoyed by America for the first 137 years in which America propelled itself to the greatest country in the world.

The greatest country ever to exist—and to think this was all accomplished *without* an income tax or *direct* tax on citizens of any kind.

For instance, few know what impact President McKinley's assassination had on the eventual passage of the resolution that provided the ignition point for a direct tax on Americans laborers. (Have they even ever been taught?) Fewer still likely know that the Republican Party, which controlled both houses of Congress in 1908, adopted what they thought was a "poison pill" to thwart its passage, only to have it backfire on them in an embarrassing fashion.

Did you know two of the four presidents on Mount Rushmore openly advocated for an income tax?

How many history classes teach students that newspapers—the main source of media in the early 1900s—seized upon a growing populist view of class division and income inequality to politicize the Sixteenth Amendment's ratification process? Political newspaper cartoonists seized upon the industry titans of the day as "robber barons" and all businessmen and entrepreneurs as "men of evil."

Probably more frightening than any conspiracy theory from *The Deep State* is where the idea of taxing one's labor and income originated. The progressive direct income tax, the major source of revenue for the United States today, is the brainchild of the Father of Communism, Karl Marx. And, a progressive income tax is the second major tenet of *The Communist Manifesto*.[5] How many public schools or universities teach that? Populist politicians knew how to gauge the wind of discontent, and the Progressive Era was born.

The primary source of funding for our federal government has really been derived from a radical Marxist ideal. Let that sink in for a moment. In how many history or civics classes do you remember learning that the majority of America's federal government revenue is extracted and modeled from *The Communist Manifesto?* "None," is likely your answer. Here's a passage from Chapter II: "Nevertheless, in the most advanced countries, the following will be pretty generally applicable. 1—Abolition of (private) property in land and application of all rents of land to public purposes. 2—A heavy progressive or graduate income tax. 3—Abolition of all right of inheritance...."[5]

The creation of the income tax was not the result of a national calamity, general emergency, or a war. Politicians of the day were actually embarrassed the government was operating in a cash surplus.[6] In 1912, the federal government's budget surplus was approximately $3 million, which is equivalent to inflation today (2018) to $77.4 billion.[7,8] It was very clear then—as it is now—that the income tax was invented principally for social change and is the crowning achievement of American progressive socialism.

In later chapters, you'll see the income tax was *never* about revenue. (However, it was a convenient source to tap into and increase rates for two world wars and dozens of other conflicts.) The income tax was designed for social change and redistribution.[9]

Besides the social changes inflicted over the years by the income tax, consider the economic impact over time to the average American citizen:

In 1913, the per capita federal debt for Americans was $31.62 per person. (Using inflation statistics, that amount equals to approximately $796.00 per capita today.)[6,8] Yet, with this new source of revenue to tap into, surely the federal government would continue to run a surplus—right? Not hardly....

In ten short years, the per capita federal government debt for Americans in 1923 grew by 384 percent to $3,060 in today's numbers.[6,8] Yes, the country had to pay for World War I; however, tax rates saw significant increases during the war—and yet, Congress didn't lower them back to pre-war levels once it was over, as they had promised.

The average revenue (taxes) the government derived per person in 1913 was $7.74 ($191.64 with today's numbers). In ten years, it had grown 465 percent to $891 per person using inflation.[6,8] Yet, you say, "But, I paid much, much more than that in taxes." Welcome to *redistribution*! The ability to extract more taxes from one citizen over another is a significant Constitutional question we will discuss in a later chapter.

Using the most current numbers available, the combined effect of having this never-ending fountain of revenue called the income tax has not materialized into gigantic surpluses for the government. The average federal debt per person in the United States in 2018 was $62,034—a mind-boggling, inflation-adjusted 7,793 percent jump from the date the Sixteenth Amendment was ratified.[6]

How is it that the government collects more money than it ever has from its American citizens; yet, the national debt is bigger than it's ever been? As of the writing of this book, the federal government had record tax revenue.[9]

The average tax revenue derived per person through the income tax has grown to an inflation-adjusted $11,232 each—a whopping 5,861 percent increase since this so-called brilliant scheme was laid on the American citizenry.[8] Let those numbers sink in for a moment.

Through a seemingly "harmless" act, Congress enacted a mechanism in which to draw huge sums of money from the populace. The progressives in both parties now had a constant source of revenue to manipulate to achieve their social change goals for the country. And, Americans that were either hell-bent on punishing the rich or apathetic to a misguided Congress let it happen. And, it continues today with the trumpeting of so-called major tax reform, which is essentially *lipstick on a pig* and hardly a fix for what is really unconstitutional per the original intent of *no direct taxation* by our Founders.

Every politician since has moseyed up to the federal revenue trough that is the income tax code for loopholes, carve-outs, subsidies, and other appropriations in order to appear the hero when they bring a small portion of what was stolen by Washington originally back home in pork-barrel spending. Notwithstanding the intent of the Founders or the arguments that several states' ratification of the Sixteenth Amendment was not done properly, it is clear direct taxes on citizens were specifically *not* allowed in the U.S. Constitution. Yet, Americans are faced with the unenviable task of, once again, amending the Constitution (which invokes separate perils to be discussed later) or completely overhauling our tax system. In this day of hyper-partisan politics, out-of-control spending, and political gridlock, Americans must figure out a permanent fix before the system crashes down upon itself with the weight of unsustainable spending, debt, and over-taxation.

Over the years, the income tax has grown into a weaponized instrument for punishing political enemies and shaping social behaviors, and it's the cash cow for the incredible growth of an inefficient, bloated, centralized government that is involved in every aspect of our lives.

American Patriots such as Thomas Jefferson, George Washington, Patrick Henry, Samuel Adams, and many others are turning over in their graves.

What can be done about it?

What will *you* do about it?

2

PROGRESSIVISM & THE ROOTS OF
AMERICAN CLASS WARFARE

"Karl Marx is the most assigned economist in U.S. college classes."

—Tom Bemis, Author
Marketwatch
January 31, 2016

Shortly after the Civil War, the United States of America entered into the Second Industrial Revolution.[1] Many historians also call that period during the late 1800s the Gilded Age.

But, before one can understand the impact of the industrialization of the country, it is essential to understand who planted the seeds of progressivism in the United States and allowed them to bear fruit over the next fifty years after the Civil War.

Progressivism was originally cast in Europe but spread rapidly to America and has been growing steadily—first making an appearance during the War Between the States and then in the early 1900s.

The progressive socialists had a "hero in precedent" in Abraham Lincoln, who had exchanged letters with Karl Marx and obviously read Marx.[2] Under Lincoln, many Constitutional doctrines were swept away with the stroke of his ink pen, including instituting an unconstitutional direct income tax and canceling the writ of habeas corpus, which, under the Constitution, forbids arrest of citizens without due process:

> On July 1, 1862, Lincoln signed a tax bill that filled more than seventeen triple-column pages of very fine print. The bill contained 119 different sections, imposing hundreds of excise taxes, stamp taxes, inheritance taxes, gross receipts taxes, and licenses taxes on virtually every occupation, service, and commodity in the entire economy. Congressman Vallandigham once again protested, and once again Thaddeus Stevens, Lincoln's point man in the Congress, branded all dissenters as traitors with the implicit threat of imprisonment.[3]

Congressman Clement Vallandigham, a Democrat from Ohio, was eventually imprisoned and then exiled to the Confederacy by Lincoln under his newfound freedom to imprison politicians, newspaper columnists, and citizens who were against his policies:

> An internal revenue bureaucracy was created within the Treasury Department for the first time. Taxation on a scale never before seen in the United States was imposed on the population of the North. Most of these taxes remained in place after the war, as did the internal revenue bureaucracy, so that every American citizen would forever have direct contact with the federal government.[3]

Lincoln may be canonized as the Great Emancipator, but he is also the father of massive centralization of power in the federal government or, as some label him, the Great Centralizer:

> The American public was also relentlessly propagandized by the government and its private sector accomplices, such as Jay Cooke (banker, Union financier, railroad tycoon), into believing that it could now look to the federal government for solutions to its problems. This made it easier for future generations of politicians to convince the American public to acquiesce in further expansions of government and

further restrictions on personal liberty that would have caused the Founding Fathers to reach for their swords.[3]

THE CONDITION OF THE LABORING MAN AT PULLMAN.—

In the late 1800s, the American economy began to slowly shift from an agrarian-type economy to a more industrialized one with larger urban populations. Inventions such as the Bessemer process for the large-scale production of steel, the telegraph and telephone, automobiles, agricultural machinery, screw propeller-driven ships, rubber, the proliferation of machined parts, drilling for petroleum and other chemicals, modern advances in electricity, urban sewage and water systems, and, of course, the growth of railroad infrastructures represented seismic shifts in daily American life.

During this growth period, the mechanization of industry led to a class of workers that were mostly unskilled. Burgeoning factories needed unskilled laborers to perform repetitive and largely simple tasks that were overseen by engineers but needed no specialized knowledge or education to be performed effectively.

The rise of a new and alternative anti-culture to this increased industrialization was taking hold in Europe, begun by Jean-Jacques Rosseau, Karl Marx, and Frederick Engels. Capitalism was effectively destroying the old feudal systems and nobility that had defined class struggles.

According to Paul Brians, PhD, an economist from Washington State University:

> The Industrial Revolution had many profound effects on European civilization. It rendered much of the old aristocracy irrelevant, boosted the bourgeoisie to economic and political power, and drafted much of the old peasant class into its factories. The result was naturally a shift in attitude toward wealth. Capitalist wealth seemed to have no natural limits. Partly because the new industrial modes of production had no preassigned place in feudal order of things, the industrialists viewed themselves as the creators of their wealth and considered it something to be proud of.[4]

This increase in the mechanization of major industries led to major industrial centers in the Northeast and the Midwest Rust Belt, thus creating job openings in manufacturing plants that drew populations from rural and Southern states eager to get jobs. The era of small-town proprietors such as the local blacksmith, wagon maker, butcher, tailor, and other skilled professions was slowly being replaced by machined parts, automobiles, trains, meat-packing plants, and garment factories.

During this era, entrepreneurs who figured out how to successfully develop methods for mass production became wealthy beyond the common citizen's wildest imaginations. Never in history had Americans been exposed to the type of wealth many industrialists and financiers of industry were experiencing. In the past, most wealthy families had taken generations to accumulate their fortunes. In almost all cases, wealth was largely determined by the amount of cattle or land owned or by the number of acres harvested. And, in many cases, the local banker was the richest man in town.

In the eighteenth century and the first half of the nineteenth century, an American citizen commonly knew who the wealthiest family was in their county, and it rarely changed. The richest family in the county when you were born was normally the richest family in the county when you died. Most local wealth continued to stay in the same families as farms, businesses, and ranches were passed down to each generation.

With the advent of these mass accumulations of wealth that occurred in less than one generation, America began to change socially. What some saw as "Captains of Industry," others saw as "robber barons."[4]

Brians goes on to state: "Many 19th-Century socialists rejected the argument that the wealthy deserve their wealth because they have created it, instead believing that wealth is created by the working classes and wrongfully appropriated by the rich who benefit disproportionately from their underpaid labor."[4]

15

This is essentially the Karl Marx theory of economics.

Several economic bubbles in the late 1800s in the U.S. burst as this new industrial revolution was gaining traction. During this period, several large industries consolidated into *trusts*, effectively creating quasi-monopolies. This led to the Sherman Anti-Trust Act of 1890, which broke up industries that had become uncompetitive by large mergers.

But, by then, the die was cast. The American newspaper media and politicians seized an opportunity to frame the Sherman Act as a check on the robber barons and evil trusts.

If you couldn't find a job in 1890—or any period up until early 1920s—it was the fault of big business. This was also the period labor unions begin forming. Money entered the political process in a manner and quantity never before seen in American politics. The Left (big labor) and the Right (big business) both cozied up to politicians who were all too eager to participate financially in the new version of American politics and influence.

The Spanish-American War saw the passage of the War Revenue Act of 1898. In this act, corporate income taxes were levied on the sugar and oil industries, and the nation saw an interesting twist to the Inheritance Tax, or Estate Tax, as we know it today.

Knowing full well that an inheritance tax is a direct tax, Congress rewrote the law ingeniously to style it as a *transfer tax* on the estate itself, and not on the citizens inheriting it. Thus, a large estate or a simple family farm paid this transfer tax in order to pass the assets of the estate to the heirs. Opponents fought this inheritance tax scheme all the way to the Supreme Court.[5]

As with many other Supreme Court decisions regarding direct taxes, in this landmark case of *Knowlton v. Moore* (1900), the Supreme Court interpreted the winds of social change being flamed by politicians and newspapers to agree with the argument that it was, in fact, a transfer tax and not a direct tax (proving the point that the Supreme Court can be political).[6] The government and progressives also never let a good crisis go to waste, as they both seized on the patriotism during wartime to advance the argument for paying your fair share. The sinking of the *USS Maine* in Havana was the perfect opportunity. Conservatives considered the levy of progressive rates of inheritance taxes to be an assault on private property rights.[6]

In this decision, Justice White claimed "...that an inheritance tax was constitutional but asserted that it was to be imposed with reference to the whole amount of personal property of which legacies and distributive shares arose."[6]

Justice McKenna in his dissent to Court's majority opinion of the application of this tax as a transfer (and without the benefit of making the inheritance tax with progressive rates) was echoed by the liberals of the time in Sydney Ratner's book *American Taxation*: "The economic consequence of Justice White's interpretation of the War Revenue Act was that the Treasury lost millions of dollars which otherwise might have been realized, and the centralization of wealth was not counteracted to the extent that Congress had desired."[7]

He maintained the act could not "be otherwise interpreted without defeating the intent of Congress."[7]

The decision would begin to define the federal government's future policy of appropriating or confiscating an increasingly large part of the property left by so-called wealthy decedents for the expenses of government.

By 1902 and the end of the short war, the treasury had a surplus of funds, and the Republicans controlled both the House and the Senate. Because of this, the presidency forced passage of a bill in Congress to end the War Revenue Act of 1898, to the outcry of the Democrats and progressives.

The distinction of the intent of direct taxes on Americans by the progressives becomes more and more evident, as Ratner writes:

> If democracy survives, it will be because the greatest good of the greatest number supplants "my good, and that of my class." In such a progressive state, as we have said, the benefits received from governmental expenditures will usually equal or exceed the deprivation caused by the payment of taxes. Taxes will pay not only for the maintenance of civil government, justice, police, the fostering of industry and commerce, but also for the

17

expenditures designed to combat business depressions and to wage wars considered necessary or just.[7]

It is abundantly clear that from its very beginning, the idea of direct taxation on citizens was not about revenue but a social redesign.

3

★

TEDDY ROOSEVELT:

THE PROGRESSIVE'S TROJAN HORSE

"A great democracy has got to be progressive or it will soon cease to be great or a democracy."

—Teddy Roosevelt (1858–1919)
26th President of the United States
Winner of 1906 Nobel Peace Prize
Congressional Medal of Honor

I t's hard not to admire Teddy Roosevelt. After all, for many historians, he is considered one of the best presidents in U.S. history. He's even memorialized on Mount Rushmore with Washington, Jefferson, and Lincoln.

During what is commonly called the Progressive Era, from 1890 to 1920, Roosevelt stands as the most significant figure in progressivism's growing popularity. Roosevelt was exceptionally popular with the public even before he became president. Much like Ulysses S. Grant, Roosevelt capitalized on his war hero status as a Rough Rider charging up San Juan Hill in the Spanish-American War. Roosevelt was the quintessential Renaissance man, whose flair for the dramatic and opportune publicity stunts set a new standard that politicians work to emulate to this day.

Stunned by his growing populist popularity and his progressive stance on many issues that angered conservative Republicans in the late 1800s and early 1900s, the GOP thought they had found a great place to shelve Roosevelt where he could do the least amount of harm. They placed him on the ballot as the vice-presidential candidate with William J. McKinley to assure a winning presidential ticket.

Roosevelt was a tireless and effective campaigner, and McKinley knew it. McKinley's Vice President Garrett Hobart died of natural causes late in McKinley's first term, paving the way for Roosevelt. In addition to Roosevelt's adroit campaigning skills, he represented everything Hobart wasn't to the growing legions of progressives in both parties.

Hobart was an attorney with strong ties to railroad trusts. The vice president's role near the turn of the century was described as the "fifth wheel to the executive coach"; however, Hobart tried to be more involved with the passage of legislation that didn't require a tiebreaking vote.[1]

Paradoxically, when Roosevelt ran for reelection in 1904, he managed to build a coalition of farmers and laborers that were more commonly aligned with Democrats; although, his main financial backers were Wall Street firms and New York financiers.[2] The model—where progressive socialists want to appear to be for the common man or woman, yet take huge amounts of campaign funds from wealthy donors—was perfected by Republican candidate Teddy Roosevelt. And, make no mistake about it, Roosevelt was a progressive. The Republican Party had a wolf by the ears that they dared not let go.

Roosevelt outmaneuvered the Democrats easily in 1904, and again in 1908, by stealing their progressive thunder. The electorate found him a champion of the common man, but the eastern Republican conservatives were aghast. Roosevelt had almost singlehandedly created a progressive wing of the Republican Party, which resulted in a divided and acrimonious party.

Ratner writes: "Dissatisfaction led to a rebellion against the vested interests and to an attempt at governmental and economic reorganization, which took on the character of a crusade for social justice."[2]

On July 4, 1906, Roosevelt announced support for a graduated income and inheritance tax at the dedication for the new House of

Representatives building.[3] Roosevelt's rhetoric for a progressive income tax became the main rallying cry for the Progressive Era.

As Roosevelt advanced through his first term as president at forty-two, the youngest age for a president in history, his pursuit of a progressive agenda was steadfast. Roosevelt made gains in needed areas—areas in which the Republicans had dropped the ball or had shamelessly protected special interests or big monopolies. Roosevelt won much-needed improvements in sanitary conditions at meat-packing plants, enforcement of child labor laws, and won the Nobel Peace Prize for negotiating an end to the Russo-Japanese War.

His regular, informal meetings with the press at the White House during his daily shaves and haircuts were the precursor to the presidential press conference and the establishment of a White House press corps. Roosevelt negotiated the end to a debilitating national coal strike as one of his first duties after inheriting the presidency upon McKinley's death.

In the presidential elections, a popular Roosevelt won fairly easily, but his party was nervous. Roosevelt prided himself on taking the wind out of the Democrats by stealing their progressive thunder. He won in an electoral college landslide (336–104) with over 2.5 million popular votes. As time progressed, Roosevelt seemed more at war with the conservatives in the GOP than the Democrats.

Burton W. Folsom with the Foundation for Economic Education writes:

> Roosevelt's quest for "a real democracy" and for centralizing power was a clear break with the American Founders. James Madison, for example, distrusted both democracy and human nature; he believed that separating power was essential to good government. He urged in Federalist No. 51 that "those who administer each department" of government be given "the necessary constitutional means and personal motives to resist the encroachments of other.... Ambition must be made to check ambition." If power was dispersed, Madison concluded, liberty might prevail and the republic might endure.[4]

Roosevelt continued to push for progressive reforms and became an unabashed promoter of the unconstitutional income tax. Folsom writes further:

> The shift from the individual rights of the Founders to the community rights of the Progressives was a watershed transition in American thought in the early 1900s. But, Roosevelt needed a federal income tax to help him redistribute wealth in the national interest. The title "New Nationalism" reflected his view that he and other leaders could determine the national interest and redistribute wealth and power accordingly.
>
> Of the income tax, Roosevelt said, "The really big fortune, the swollen fortune, by the mere fact of its size, acquires qualities which differentiate it in kind as well as in degree from what is possessed by men of relatively small means. Therefore, I believe in a graduated income tax on big fortunes, and in another tax which is far more easily collected and far more effective—a graduated inheritance tax on big fortunes, properly safeguarded against evasion, and increasing rapidly in amount with the size of the estate."[4]

Roosevelt had no qualms about openly calling for an unconstitutional, direct, and progressive income tax, stating on April 14, 1906:

> It is important to this people to grapple with the problems connected with the amassing of enormous fortunes, and the use of those fortunes, both corporate and individual, in business. We should discriminate in the sharpest way between fortunes well-won and fortunes ill-won; between those gained as an incident to performing great services to the community as a whole, and those gained in evil fashion by keeping just within the limits of mere law-honesty.[5]

Roosevelt played on the evil robber barons, once again fomenting the public thought that successful entrepreneurs could only get that way by taking advantage of the poor. He continues:

I feel that we shall ultimately have to consider the adoption of some such scheme as that of a progressive tax on all fortunes, beyond a certain amount either given in life or devised or bequeathed upon death to any individual—a tax so framed as to put it out of the power of the owner of one of these enormous fortunes to hand on more than a certain amount to any one individual; the tax, of course, to be imposed by the National and not the State Government. Such taxation should, of course, be aimed merely at the inheritance or transmission in their entirety of those fortunes swollen beyond all healthy limits.[5]

Thus, the likable American hero of San Juan Hill and the champion of the "everyman" not only gave instant credibility in the American public eye about adapting a foundational tenant of Marxism but became its leading advocate. The following year, Roosevelt delivers these remarks to Congress on December 7, 1907:

When our tax laws are revised the question of an income tax and an inheritance tax should receive the careful attention of our legislators. In my judgment both of these taxes should be part of our system of Federal taxation. I speak diffidently about the income tax because one scheme for an income tax was declared unconstitutional by the Supreme Court; while in addition it is a difficult tax to administer in its practical working, and great care would have to be exercised to see that it was not evaded by the very men whom it was most desirable to have taxed, for if so evaded it would, of course, be worse than no tax at all; as the least desirable of all taxes is the tax which bears heavily upon the honest as compared with the dishonest man. Nevertheless, a graduated income tax of the proper type would be a desirable feature of Federal taxation, and it is to be hoped that one may be devised which the Supreme Court will declare constitutional.... The Government has the absolute right to decide as to the terms upon which a man shall receive a bequest or devise from another, and this point in the devolution of property is especially appropriate for the imposition of a tax.[5]

As you can see, Roosevelt concluded his speech to Congress with an alarming assault on private property rights by echoing Marx's abolishment of private property—in this case, a citizen's right to bequeath his wealth as he or she sees fit.

In his New Nationalism speech in Kansas in 1910, we can further see how Roosevelt equates the accumulation of wealth to a slave-holding plantation owner:

> At many stages in the advance of humanity, this conflict between the men who possess more than they have earned and the men who have earned more than they possess is the central condition of progress. In our day it appears as the struggle of freemen to gain and hold the right of self-government as against the special interests, who twist the methods of free government into machinery for defeating the popular will. At every stage, and under all circumstances, the essence of the struggle is to equalize opportunity, destroy privilege, and give to the life and citizenship of every individual the highest possible value both to himself and to the commonwealth. That is nothing new. All I ask in civil life is what you fought for in the Civil War. I ask that civil life be carried on according to the spirit in which the army was carried on. You never get perfect justice, but the effort in handling the army was to bring to the front the men who could do the job. Nobody grudged promotion to Grant, or Sherman, or Thomas, or Sheridan, because they earned it. The only complaint was when a man got a promotion which he did not earn.[6]

Roosevelt directly states reference to those "who possess more than they have earned...." Take Roosevelt's name off this speech, and it very well could have been written and delivered by Karl Marx.

Although though no law was enacted to prevent a U.S. president for serving more than two terms until after Franklin D. Roosevelt (FDR married Teddy's niece) served three terms, Teddy

Roosevelt had promised not to run for a third. It was politically accepted that no U.S. president would serve more than two, and since Teddy had served 3.5 years of McKinley's term after his assassination, he promised when running in 1904 that it would be his last time.

ELEVEN HOURS A DAY

Roosevelt handpicked William H. Taft as his successor. With Roosevelt's endorsement, Taft easily beat Democrat William Jennings Bryan, who had lost for the third time as the Democratic nominee for president. Taft was more conservative than Roosevelt. To Roosevelt's dismay, after being elected, he openly sided with business interests and the conservative wing of the GOP during his single term in office.

Dissatisfied with the conservatism of his successor, Taft, and the rate of progressive reforms during Taft's administration, Roosevelt entered the 1912 Republican nomination late and could not overcome Taft's party machinery—they had a significant head start as the incumbent, and maintained a slim lead and ultimately won the nomination.

Despite the outcry for splitting the vote from the dysfunctional GOP, Roosevelt entered the presidential race as an independent, establishing the Bull Moose Party. This resulted in the Republican vote nationwide being split, handing the presidency to progressive Democrat Woodrow Wilson in an electoral landslide (438–88), carrying forty states but only 41 percent of the popular vote.[7]

The two Republicans, Roosevelt (27.4 percent) and Taft (23.2 percent), won more popular votes collectively than Wilson (50.6 percent).[7] If not for the split, caused by Roosevelt, the Republicans would have likely carried the 1912 election, and, thus, prevented Woodrow Wilson—viewed by many conservatives as one of our worst presidents—from winning. Wilson gave us the ratification of the Sixteenth and Seventeenth Amendments, as well as the Federal Reserve Act, and he entered the U.S. into World War I.

Additionally, and of particular note in this election, was Socialist Party candidate Eugene V. Debs. He won six percent of the popular vote, representing almost one million voters.[7] By 1912, the Socialist Party had over 100,000 members.[8]

The Progressive Era, championed by Teddy Roosevelt, had firmly taken hold of U.S. politics and the will of the American people. It was only a matter of time—a few years, in this case—that Americans would begin to lose their Liberty through the Sixteenth Amendment.

4

★

CONSTITUTIONAL TAXES

"Before the income tax was foisted upon us, it was accepted without question that his home is his castle. Now, he and his home and his offices have the privacy of a goldfish bowl."

—Vivien Kellems (1896–1975)
American Industrialist & Entrepreneur
Champion of the Equal Rights Amendment
Woman's Suffrage Leader & Activist

To understand what the Founders intended when framing the U.S. Constitution, it is vitally important to know what they absolutely *didn't* want. The colonists had just fought an eight-year war for independence from a monarchy that imposed highly unpopular taxes via the Stamp Act and various other duties, including a tax on tea.

The Articles of Confederation were purposely drawn and ratified by the colonies to put very restrictive powers on the federal government, including the power to tax. Although the Articles of Confederation allowed for the creation of the Continental Army for the Revolutionary War, it had to summon the individual states for money to keep the Army provisioned.

At that time, the only power to raise money through taxation was the legislature of each state. American colonists detested taxation because of what they went through with the English king and parliament. They were loath to send tax money to any central power.[1]

When the Constitutional Convention convened, there was heavy debate about taxation to fund the limited and enumerated powers granted in the Constitution. Specifically, the Constitution addressed the power of the federal government to tax as follows:

- Article I, Section 2: Representatives and direct Taxes shall be <u>apportioned</u> among the several states which may be included in this Union, according to their respective Numbers....
- Article I, Section 9: <u>No Capitation, or other direct Tax</u> shall be laid, unless in Proportion to the Census or enumeration herein before directed to be taken.[2]

Originally, the costs of maintaining a federal government and for providing revenue to carry out whatever enumerated powers granted to the federal government were to be *apportioned* or divided equally among the states according to their census population. It was then up to each state legislature to raise the funds for their pro rata (or apportioned) share of the cost of the federal government. With this type of system, it was very easy for state legislators to control the growth of the federal government and its spending. Additionally, the cost of the federal government was very simple to determine and was completely transparent to citizens.

During the Constitutional Convention of 1787, it was determined that the Articles of Confederation had not delivered a reliable source of revenue with which to fund the government. Many states did not convene legislatures on a regular basis, and some voted not to send *any* money to the federal government.

Popular written opinion articles known as *The Federalist Papers* were widely distributed in the states during this period in newspapers, broadsides, and pamphlets authored by Alexander Hamilton, John Jay, and James Madison to promote a better understanding of the Constitution and to promote its ratification. But, even in these papers, Hamilton and Madison disagreed in many areas and took their debate to the public via these publications.

For instance, James Madison (with significant influence from Patrick Henry and the Anti-Federalists) was the author of the Bill of Rights, which Hamilton vociferously opposed in *The Federalist Papers*. Madison was also the originator of the systems of checks and balances between the three branches of government. Hamilton came up with the Supremacy Clause and the Necessary and Proper Clause—which has been widely and loosely interpreted and arguably abused according to various opinions in the Supreme Court in recent years.

Concern ran high during the Convention that the states would break apart if a stronger Constitution did not replace the Articles of Confederation. Most Founding Fathers struggled with a "supreme" centralized federal authority and believed they had drafted a Constitution of *negative powers*, meaning that the federal government was limited in what it could do but was mostly written with specific actions it could not take—or those reserved only for the states.

Writing in contrast to Hamilton's "Federalist No. 51," the Anti-Federalists led by Patrick Henry had genuine concerns about Hamilton's influence in the Constitution. The chief concern of the Anti-Federalists was that the executive powers of the president were too strong, that the judiciary would eventually be out of control, and that a national government would be too far away from the people and, thus, unresponsive to the needs of localities.[3]

In particular, these Founders had legitimate concerns about the "general welfare" clause when it came to raising taxes or spending taxpayers' money.

Referring to Brutus VI (Hamilton's "Federalist No. 6"), the Anti-Federalists write:

> A power that has such latitude, which reaches every person in the community in every conceivable circumstance, and lays hold of every species of property they possess, and which has no bounds set to it, but the discretion of those who exercise it, I say, such a power must necessarily, from its very nature, swallow up all the power of the state governments.

I would ask those, who reason thus, to define what ideas are included under the terms, to provide for the common defence and general welfare? Are these terms definite, and will they be understood in the same manner, and to apply to the same cases by everyone? No one will pretend they will. It will then be matter of opinion, what tends to the general welfare; and the Congress will be the only judges in the matter. To provide for the general welfare, is an abstract proposition, which mankind differ in the explanation of, as much as they do on any political or moral proposition that can be proposed;

It is as absurd to say, that the power of Congress is limited by these general expressions, "to provide for the common safety, and general welfare," as it would be to say, that it would be limited, had the constitution said they should have power to lay taxes, &c. at will and pleasure.

The government would always say, their measures were designed and calculated to promote the public good; and there being no judge between them and the people, the rulers themselves must, and would always, judge for themselves.[4]

Their concerns, as it turns out, were well justified, looking at the ability today of a president to engage in foreign conflicts or for judges to legislate from the bench, and considering the rampant detachment of a huge, centralized government from Main Street U.S.A.

The Anti-Federalists, along with Thomas Jefferson and James Madison, formed the Democratic-Republican Party (the forerunner of the Republican Party) and opposed the centralizing policies under the Federalist Party ran by Alexander Hamilton. The Democratic-Republican Party would much later (1825) splinter with Andrew Jackson, who formed the Democratic Party.

Several states would not ratify the Constitution without the Bill of Rights added, but, once those were adopted, it was finally ratified in 1787.

America's sole source of federal government revenue for the next seventy-four years was derived from import tariffs, duties, and excise taxes. These were considered indirect taxes, which did not need to be apportioned. In this system of taxation, similar to the Articles of Confederation, American citizens could easily see the duties and excise taxes they paid. These import tariffs helped American industry and funded the government and military. If someone didn't want to pay them, he or she simply didn't purchase those imports or conduct any transaction that included an excise tax.

Several states adopted inheritance taxes with varying degrees of success, which would eventually also be challenged in the Supreme Court as a direct tax.

In 1861, Abraham Lincoln and Congress passed the first income tax in an effort to finance the Union's war efforts. Lincoln, who had already taken certain actions that were in violation of the Constitution in the name of a national calamity, championed the passage of the War Revenue Act of 1861.[5] Although the first American income tax was a single flat-rate marginal tax levied over a certain amount of income (as the federal government would increase many times over), only a year passed before tinkering with the newfound revenue source. The very next year, in 1862, Lincoln and Congress increased the tax rates and added a graduated or *progressive* component to the income tax—and, for good measure, added a federal estate or inheritance tax.

On August 5, 1861, the *New York Times* praised the new tax law: "Millionaires like Mr. W.B. Astor, Commodore Vanderbilt and others, will henceforth contribute a fair proportion of their wealth to the support of the national government."[6]

This is one of the very first public statements in America that uses progressive income inequality and a "soak the rich" mentality.

The sleight of hand that Congress uses on a frequent basis to fool their constituents has been mastered by both parties over the years. Even the *New York Times* recognized the hastily drawn and intentional misdirection of the direct tax bill championed by Lincoln in a November 10, 1861 edition that states:

An act to provide increased revenue from imports, to pay interest on the public debt, and for other purposes. The chapter covers twenty pages, yet less than three contain all that relates to import duties, and the remaining seventeen are devoted to subject not even hinted at the heading, viz.; to the direct and income taxes. This omission in the caption is, of itself, an error unworthy of the National Legislature, since it evinces hast and carelessness; but is trifling in comparison with those which followed.[7]

The following *New York Times* article, also written in 1861, is, perhaps, the clearest argument in my research that explains the farce that is the income tax when taken into constitutional context. The journalist also has a knack for displaying the elitism and incompetence that existed in Congress (yes, even in 1861):

The first article of the Constitution declares that: Representation and direct taxation shall be apportioned among the several States which may be included within this Union, according to their respective numbers.... No capitation or other direct tax shall be laid, unless in proportion to the census or enumeration herein before directed to be taken.

[The proposed tax as written] shall be levied, collected and paid upon the annual income of every person residing in the United States, whether such income is derived from any kind of property, or from any profession, trade, employment or vocation carried on in the United States or elsewhere, or from any other source whatever, if such annual income exceeds the sum of eight hundred dollars, a tax of three per centum on the of such excess of such income above eight hundred dollars.

[In comes the *Times'* most damning claims.]

It is seen that this income tax imposes the same uniform per centum upon the profits of all citizens of the United States, and thus entirely ignores the principle of Federal numbers, and the varying proportions of tax due from the several States.... It is sweeping in its terms, and goes on to provide for the appointment of collectors and to bind them up in heavy penalties to exact the last farthing, without reference to the State quotas. In truth, the act is indefinite as to the amount to be collected, and it was therefore impossible to apportion the State their quotas, according to federal numbers. It must be obvious that the failure to apportion the income tax among the States according to their federal numbers, defined in the Constitution, is a mistake which vitiates the act in all its parts, and renders it consistent with that instrument; but behind this there is another error, radical in its character, which renders apportionment impossible, and that is the omission to the name the sum to be raised. The land-tax law very properly sets out with a requisition of twenty million dollars, and a

33

definite state of the quota of each State. The income-tax law, on the contract sets no limit to the amount of revenue to be raised under it, but requires from all citizens of the United States a uniform three per centum of their incomes, when the amount shall exceed a given sum.[7]

Notice, the amount needed to run the government is mentioned first, and apportioning it to the states is secondary. Stating federal revenue requirements before setting excise taxes or import duties had been custom. Here, we see the very first American income tax leave the "amount to be raised" by a direct income tax totally unlimited. Furthermore, the *Times* article goes on to excoriate the body as an elitist cadre of self-interest exhibited in Congress that would seem like today's modern politicians:

> The provision of the income tax commences, and here the law-makers seem to have totally lost sight of the Constitution in their patriotic fervor, or more probably, their eagerness to get home. It may seem surprising that 300 men of average intelligence should all simultaneously have become oblivious of some of the plainest provisions of the fundamental law…. But to those who have been in the habit of attending to the mode of doing business in the capital, and who are aware that no member ever thinks of reading a bill, or listening to its reading, unless he happens to belong to the committee which reports it, the mystery is easy of explication. The three formal readings in the presence of the houses, which the parliamentary rules require every bill to undergo before becoming a law, are the most shameful farces. In the first place, two [of] the readings have been reduced in practice to nothing more than an announcement of the bills by their headings, while the one actual reading, which the clerk performs at 2.40 speed, amid loud talking, boisterous laughing and general uproar, no man is eccentric as to think of paying attention.[7]

The Supreme Court case *Springer v. United States* (1881) later challenged this original American income tax and inexplicably ruled the income tax was, in fact, not a direct tax but an excise tax. Although the income tax had expired in 1873, the plaintiff was still dealing with its aftereffects as his home and farm were confiscated and sold for amounts the tax collector had determined were due.[8]

The plaintiff in this case also argued for due process, a basic Constitutional right that was not afforded him before confiscation occurred. This was an oft-cited precedence case for excusing the government from providing due process before the tax was paid. The question of the constitutionality of the income tax did not come up again until 1894.[8]

In 1894, the Democrats wanted to reduce the import tariff duties imposed by the 1890 McKinley tariff, and they inserted a two percent income tax on incomes over $4,000 (a figure with inflation well over $150,000 in 2018)[9] to make up the lost revenue that occurred from lowering the tariffs. This act was titled the Wilson-Gorman Tariff, passed easily in the democratically controlled House and Senate, and was signed by President Grover Cleveland.[10]

On February 10, 1894, the headline in the Saturday evening edition of *The Globe* (New York) reads "A Week's Income—The Millionaires Could Pay Uncle Sam's Tax in Seven Days—Drops in Buckets, Would John R. Rockefeller Miss It from $7.6M per Year?"[11]

Even here, we see the progressives denote how Rockefeller "wouldn't miss" the amount of money he paid in taxes—as if the government is entitled to Rockefeller's earnings. The article goes on to list several dozen New York City area millionaires and what their "paltry" tax bills would be. Of course, the justification is they didn't earn it, so they wouldn't miss it anyway.[11] This is the first example found in my research that involved "public shaming" of the wealthy.

In 1895, the lawsuit *Pollock v. Farmers' Loan & Trust Company* made its way through the courts and finally to the Supreme Court. In essence, Mr. Pollock was challenging the portion of the 1894 Wilson-Gorman Act that provided for the direct taxation of profits of stock investment, arguing, in brief, that direct taxes were unconstitutional and should be apportioned (by population) to the states.[12]

This landmark case was decided 5–4 in favor of Pollock, and the income tax was defeated and ruled unconstitutional. Knowing what it would eventually take to get a direct income tax permanent, and, as a result of the *Pollack* ruling, the progressive Democrats made the adoption of a Constitutional amendment to authorize a direct income tax part of their party plank at the next convention.

Although preserving the prohibition of a direct tax on income, the tax on inheritances wouldn't be as fortunate.

Later in the late 1800s, Congress figured out how to get around the designation of the inheritance tax by not taxing the beneficiaries of the inheritance, but by putting an excise tax on the value of the estate instead, although it had the same effect. It was challenged in 1899 in *Nicol v. Ames*[13], and again in 1900, in *Knowlton v. Moore*.[14] Eventually, it became permanent with the passage of the Sixteenth Amendment.

5

★

THE GOP'S GRAND MISTAKE

"When plunder becomes a way of life for a group of men in a society, over the course of time they create for themselves a legal system that authorizes it and a moral code that glorifies it."

—Frédéric Bastiat (1801–1850)
French Economist
Defender of Individual Liberties
Opposed Government-Sponsored Redistribution

The Progressive Era, which had begun in 1890 but really hit its stride in the early 1900s, was beginning to have an effect on public opinion regarding an income tax.

Newspapers and progressive politicians had successfully cast the immensely successful and ultra-wealthy industrialists as robber barons. The Democrats had squarely situated themselves with the common man and organized labor, pitting classes against each other. How effective it became is obvious with the success of Teddy Roosevelt, who had stolen the Democrats' thunder—and, unlike a Republican, by professing himself the champion of the people by attacking large business interests, trusts, and the ultra-wealthy.

In the meantime, the GOP failed to recognize or act upon serious issues of the times that, left unsolved, would appear to be either unbridled capitalism or the making of a plutocracy wherein only moneyed interests are protected by the government.

Examples of issues of the times that the GOP failed to address included adopting reforms to end child labor and the government turning a blind eye to or, in some cases, enabling giant monopolies to exist in rail, shipping, steel, and other industries. Those who defended Roosevelt during this era tended to elevate his attempts to call attention to these needed reforms; however, Roosevelt's drum-beating for an income tax did nothing but feed into the progressives' dogma of class warfare and, as its most prominent figure, may have actually legitimized it.

In Roosevelt's New Nationalism speech in July 1906, in dedication to the new congressional building, he professed that taxes were *patriotic* and that only a powerful federal government could regulate the economy and guarantee justice.[1,2]

In June 1907, Roosevelt declared: "Most great civilized countries have an income tax and an inheritance tax. In my judgment, both should be part of our system of federal taxation."[1]

In succeeding Roosevelt, President Taft saw the political wind change on a progressive income tax that Roosevelt had stoked for years. In January 1908, President Taft announced in his presidential address that he recommended a resolution on sending an amendment to the states on income tax—although, he and his conservative colleagues wholeheartedly believed passage of the resolution to send it to the states assured the idea of a direct income tax, a long and painful death.[1]

Shortly thereafter, a federal inheritance tax passed Congress in April 1909. Various bills and proposals for an income tax were making their way through committees with fierce resistance by a modest group of conservative congressmen and senators, but they were in the minority.

The idea of an income tax had taken root in America's lexicon and, now, the only issue was how to cure the unconstitutionality of it.

In addition to the Republican president, the GOP owned both the House and the Senate. The Republicans were about to make one of the greatest blunders in American political history, a mistake so grand that it would affect Americans for generations to come.

Taking a page from Roosevelt's political handbook and with direction from GOP leadership, many Republicans voted for the resolution with the belief it would never materialize or get ratified. Many of these Republican seats were going to be up for election the next election cycle. Most were feeling the winds of political change in the electorate—which was buying into the class warfare fed to them by the media, socialists, and university elites at the time.

The House passed the ratification resolution measure easily, with only four hours of debate in advance of a recess, where many were in a hurry to get back their districts. The Senate, with Republicans holding the super-majority of sixty Republicans, voted unanimously, 77–0, in favor of the resolution. Taft signed the bill...and the resolution to ratify the direct taxation of American citizens was now off to the states for ratification.

During the same Congress, the corporate income tax reared its head under the Payne-Aldrich Tariff Act. To circumvent the apportionment and direct tax constitutional issue, Roosevelt had initially proposed this as an "excise" tax for the privilege of doing business, meaning it wouldn't be classified as a corporate income tax. To demonstrate how anti-business this period in America was, the tax records were originally required to be made public. (Two years later, this decision was rescinded.)

That same year, the State of Virginia imposed an income tax; however, citizens refused to comply or cooperate. When tax agents traveled to rural Virginia to collect, some were never heard from again. It was repealed a year later as ineffective at raising revenue.[1]

In 1911, after the consolidation of fifteen lawsuits on the constitutionality of the corporate income tax made its way to the Supreme Court, it finally ruled in favor of the government in *Flint v. Stone Tracey Company*. The corporate income tax would be defined as an "excise" tax, justified by the Court for the *privilege* of doing business until the Sixteenth Amendment was ratified.

Alabama was the first state to ratify the Sixteenth Amendment in 1909, but it would take four more years to acquire the thirty-six states needed for ratification. The newspapers of the day made it a race and a media event to see which states would put the amendment over the top. Even the New Jersey governor called a special election to try to beat Wyoming as the state that put the ratification over the top, but Wyoming became the deciding state.

Connecticut, Rhode Island, Utah, and Virginia soundly rejected the Sixteenth Amendment. Florida and Pennsylvania never even considered the amendment for a vote.

The conservative wing of the GOP was horrified.

The newly minted Sixteenth Amendment was now the law of the land. It effectively killed the apportionment requirement and allowed for a direct tax:

XVI Amendment

The Congress shall have power to lay and collect taxes on incomes, from whatever source derived, without apportionment among the several states, and without regard to any census or enumeration.

6

★

"PAY AS YOU GO"
—A DIRECT ASSAULT ON LIBERTY

"The withholding feature of the income tax is a still more clear-cut instance of involuntary servitude.... What moral principle justifies the government's forcing employers to act as unpaid tax collectors?"

—Murray Newton Rothbard (1926–1995)
Renowned Economist, Author, & Libertarian

Vivien Kellems is an American heroine whose name is, unfortunately, not synonymous with typical female civil rights leaders of the twenty-first century. Her story is not taught in schools, nor does the average American have a clue of the heroic nature of Vivien Kellems, a woman who should be celebrated with the likes of Rosa Parks, Clara Barton, Susan B. Anthony, and Lucy Burns.

But, in 2006, George Washington University's Columbian College of Arts & Sciences championed her in an article entitled, "Vivien Kellems: Tax Resister, Feminist, Industrialist":

Already a prominent industrialist in Connecticut, she waded into the fight for the Equal Rights Amendment. In stating her case, she put forward her own brand of individualist feminism. By contrast, many "social feminists" at the time such as Eleanor Roosevelt opposed the ERA because it would strike down "protective legislation" for

41

women. In 1943, Kellems asked, "What are you going to do with all these women in industry? If we're good enough to go into these factories and turn out munitions in order to win this war, we're good enough to hold those jobs after the war and to sit at a table to determine the kind of peace that shall be made, and the kind of world we and our children are going to have in the future."

In 1948, however, Kellems took the national spotlight in the cause that would dominate the rest of her life. She refused to withhold income taxes from the paychecks of her 100 employees. The IRS retaliated by taking $8,000 from her bank account. Kellems took the feds to court arguing that because her workers had already paid their taxes personally, she should not be liable.[1]

Kellems earned a bachelor's degree from the University of Oregon and a master's from Columbia, working toward her PhD.

Kellems was a tireless supporter for Women's Suffrage and Equal Rights and used her position as a business leader to eventually win the right for women to vote.

In 1927, she founded Kellems Cable Grips in Manhattan, based on an invention by her brother, Edgar. She later moved the business to Connecticut. These products were used in the building projects for the Chrysler Building, New York subway system, and the George Washington Bridge, among others.[2]

Kellems ran for various seats in Congress and the U.S. Senate from Connecticut but never won. Her outspoken opposition to the graduated progressive and direct income tax was used by opponents to paint her as unpatriotic. Kellems was a strict constitutionalist who did not believe in the constitutionality of income tax, despite the Sixteenth Amendment.

In 1948, she announced her plans to fight the IRS publicly at a speaking event in California, which earned her an invitation to appear as the first woman ever on NBC's *Meet the Press*.[3] Kellems announced to the world that she would no longer withhold federal income taxes from her employees' paychecks. Kellems argued that the IRS did not compensate her company or reimburse her for time and trouble and that she shouldn't be doing the IRS's work for them.

Kellems pulled her employees together, told them she would not withhold their taxes, and strongly advised them to set aside their taxes each pay period, so they could pay in themselves if they felt inclined. The IRS went after Kellems unmercifully. Kellems' company paid the taxes they were required as a company, but the IRS wasn't satisfied and took her to court. After auditing all of her employees, who, to the last individual, paid all their taxes on time and correctly for the period in question, the government still wasn't satisfied.

Despite the IRS having received all monies required from both the employees and Kellems' company, Kellems was penalized for not withholding taxes from her employees—an amount that was equal to the taxes that had been paid by the employees, plus a 100-percent penalty to her firm. This instigated a series of lawsuits over several years, accumulating thousands of dollars in legal costs. Kellems was ultimately vindicated—the penalties and the 100-percent penalty were squashed—but she was still penalized for not withholding. Over the next few years and for the rest of her life, Kellems became a staunch advocate for the repeal of the Sixteenth Amendment and a defender of other American citizens who'd been denied the Bill of Rights and other due process by the IRS.[4]

The 1930s saw the progressive liberals really hitting their stride with manipulation of the income taxes. This was due to the economic depression and a looming war in Europe that looked more and more unavoidable for the United States.

To extend the IRS's reach on American citizens abroad, field offices were opened in foreign countries, the first one in the Philippines in 1936.[5]

From 1937–1947, Chairman of the New York Federal Reserve Board Beardsley Ruml was the leading proponent of the government taking the first fruits of labor through a *Pay as You Go* program. Beardsley, who had immense influence over President Hoover and President Roosevelt, is considered the father of withholding. This scheme has bamboozled Americans into "pre-

43

paying" their tax liability without actually knowing what their tax liability would be. It's ingenious—and Marxist.

In a 1946 speech given to the American Bar Association, Ruml elucidates his government's beliefs in elaborate fashion:

> The public purpose which is served should never be obscured in a tax program under the mask of raising revenue. Federal taxes can be made to serve four principal purposes of a social and economic character. These purposes are:
>
> 1. As an Instrument of fiscal policy to help stabilize the power of the dollar.
> 2. To express public policy in the distribution of wealth and income, as in the case of the progressive income and estate taxes.
> 3. To express public policy in subsidizing or in penalizing various industries and economic groups.
> 4. To isolate and assess directly the costs of certain benefits, such as highways and Social Security.
>
> Among the policy questions with which we have to deal with are these: Do we want a greater equality of wealth and of income than would result from economic forces working alone? Do we want to subsidize certain industries and certain economic groups? Do we want the beneficiaries of certain activities to be aware of what they want?[6]

Ruml's statements to the American Bar Association are uncommonly candid, stating the objective of the income tax and withholding with shocking clarity. His comments also highlight the cozy relationship between the Federal Reserve and the progressive income tax.

Congress passed the Social Security Act in 1935, and President Roosevelt signed it. It was voluntary, despite many progressives pushing for mandatory participation. In 1937, at the urging of Ruml, mandatory withholding of taxes by employers was enacted. After this extreme overreach became law, the responsibility of collecting taxes from citizens fell to the employers.

If an employer did not cooperate (similar to Vivien Kellems), the employer was subject to punitive fines and even criminal prosecution. Now that the government had their hand on the first fruits of Americans' labor, it was an easy next step to make contributions to Social Security mandatory.

The outgrowth of the Progressive Era, championed by Teddy Roosevelt, was accelerated by his cousin, Franklin D. Roosevelt, in the 1930s, as FDR used the Great Depression as the backdrop to fully engross America into this Marxist ideology.

FDR had strong opinions related to income tax and was also not bashful or embarrassed by the Marxist influences on his tax and social policies, stating: "Here is my principle: Taxes shall be levied according to ability to pay. That is the only American principle."

Even at the beginning of World War II, FDR demonstrated his subscription to progressive Marxist ideologies. In what has turned out to be a common theme in American history, liberal politicians consistently want to tie patriotism to the amount of taxes a citizen pays—or worse, wherein the state places an arbitrary ceiling on income. FDR makes this inconceivable statement in a White House news release dated April 27, 1942: "In the time of this grave national danger, when all excess income should go to win the war, no American citizen ought to have a net income, after he has paid taxes, of more than $25,000 per year."[7]

There's no doubt that, at times of national crisis, especially in war, sacrifices have to be made. However, like Lincoln in wartime before him, FDR urges Congress to adopt unconstitutional limits on citizens' freedoms—including instructions to tax the citizenry heavily, to intentionally keep corporate profits low, to control prices, and to force citizens to have deductions from their paychecks involuntarily for war bonds and rationing:

> Relying on past and present experience, and leaving out masses of details which relate more to questions of method than to the objective itself, I list for the Congress the following points, which, taken together, may well be called our present national economic policy.

1. To keep the cost of living from spiraling upward, we must tax heavily, and in that process keep personal and corporate profits at a reasonable rate, the word "reasonable" being defined at a low level.

2. To keep the cost of living from spiraling upward, we must fix ceilings on the prices which consumers, retailers, wholesalers and manufacturers pay for the things they buy; and ceilings on rents for dwellings in all areas affected by war industries.

3. To keep the cost of living from spiraling upward, we must stabilize the remuneration received by individuals for their work.

4. To keep the cost of living from spiraling upward, we must stabilize the prices received by growers for the products of their lands.

5. To keep the cost of living from spiraling upward, we must encourage all citizens to contribute to the cost of winning this war by purchasing War Bonds with their earnings instead of using those earnings to buy articles which are not essential.

6. To keep the cost of living from spiraling upward, we must ration all essential commodities of which there is a scarcity, so that they may be distributed fairly among consumers and not merely in accordance with financial ability to pay high prices for them.

7. To keep the cost of living from spiraling upward, we must discourage credit and installment buying, and encourage the paying off of debts, mortgages, and other obligations; for this promotes savings, retards excessive buying and adds to the amount available to the creditors for the purchase of War Bonds.[7]

Having won World War II, some might say second-guessing or being an "armchair quarterback" after the fact is not fair and that it took these types of measures to beat the Axis Powers. That is not the point, in my opinion. The point here is that progressives use any crisis, no matter how little or large, real or imagined, to incrementally creep into our sacred, God-given rights to Liberty and even work to steal them.

FDR goes on, like all liberals from either party, to tie these incursions into Liberty with a patriotic bow:

> In the first item, legislation is necessary, and the subject is now under consideration in the House of Representatives. Its purpose is to keep excess profits down and, at the same time, raise further large sums for the financing of the war.
>
> Profits must be taxed to the utmost limit consistent with continued production. This means all business profits—not only in making munitions, but in making or selling anything else. Under the proposed new law, we seek to take by taxation all undue or excess profits. It is incumbent upon the Congress to define undue or excess profits; and anything in excess of that specific figure should go to the Government
>
> I have been urged by many persons and groups to recommend the adoption of a compulsory plan of savings by deducting a certain percentage of everyone's income. I prefer, however, to keep the voluntary plan in effect as long as possible, and I hope for a magnificent response.[7]

What is "excess," and who defines it? This is similar to today's approach of everyone "paying their fair share." And, who is the ultimate arbiter of the amount that is considered "excess"?

FDR's Marxist tendencies reveal themselves in even more candor as he wraps up this message to Congress:

> Some have called this an "economy of sacrifice." Some interpret it in terms that are more accurate-the "equality of sacrifice." I have never been able to bring myself, however, to full acceptance of the word "sacrifice," because free men and women, bred in the concepts of democracy and wedded to the principles of democracy, deem it a privilege rather than a sacrifice to work and to fight for the perpetuation of the democratic ideal. It is, therefore, more true to call this

total effort of the American people an "equality of privilege."[7]

The federal government later terms these taxes as "Victory" taxes. It's easy to see how messages like this continue to be heard today from progressives. Paying your "fair share" of taxes becomes an "equality of privilege," and that dogma is alive and well in today's national political discourse—to the point of apathetic acceptance by the general citizenry at large.

In 1942, withholding taxes by employers became the law of the land. Again, I take you back to the Founders for introspection on how Jefferson, Madison, Henry, Clay, and others would have responded to King George III, who invoked an edict that the colonists were to give the first fruits of their labor to the Crown.

Originally, the government's argument for the new Pay as You Go system of withholding was for our benefit. We wouldn't have to save up for April 15 every year and pay a lump sum in taxes—or worse, owe money to the IRS because we had not saved up enough.

It's not uncommon for regular, working Americans to be focused on what their take-home pay is, instead of what their gross wages would be. This fact of life has completely degenerated into accepted practice. Withholding, coupled with income tax refund checks, has hidden the cost of government from the average wage earner. After someone enters into the workforce for the first time and experiences the deductions for FICA, federal income taxes, Medicare, and other mandatory deductions, the shock factor sinks into reticent acceptance for the rest of one's life.

The federal government, inept in most areas, has been extremely successful in hiding the cost of government in your taxes. Investopedia, an investment strategy website, is critical of the withholding system on several fronts:

> People don't notice the missing money. People tend to focus on their take-home pay, which makes sense since that's the amount of money they actually have to work with. And when they do look at the tax withheld, it may not seem like a significant amount, since it's divided among the 24 or so paychecks most people receive each year. Since most

people don't ever touch all the money they've earned and they only see a number for the total amount of federal tax they've paid once a year on their tax returns (which don't show how much they've also paid for Social Security and Medicare, or how much their employers have contributed to Social Security and Medicare on their behalf) it's easier for the government to collect taxes under a withholding system, even at relatively high rates.[8]

Imagine how irate Americans would be if they were paid in cash, then had to count out a portion of their hard-earned wages from their pay envelope and give it to the federal tax man waiting anxiously for his cut.

In discussing the benefits to the government for the system of withholding, Investopedia is clear why the government wants the first fruits of your labor before you even touch—or see—it:

1. Withholding increases compliance and decreases evasion and underpayment. Because of the aforementioned savings dilemma, withholding makes it more likely that the government will receive all the taxes it is due. Withholding also makes it more difficult for tax protesters and tax evaders to keep their money out of the IRS's hands.

2. Withholding decreases collection costs. Since most people have all or most of their taxes remitted to the government by their employers, the IRS theoretically has a smaller pool of people to go after for unpaid or underpaid taxes. Lucky you   this means that fewer of your tax dollars are needed to fund the IRS's collection efforts.

3. Government can use the money sooner and receives payments and thus program funding throughout the year. If this point is truly a rationale for withholding, it would seem that government is admitting that its own employees aren't very good at managing the budgets for their programs, either. If they were, it wouldn't matter if

programs were funded in a lump sum in April or with steady payments all year long.[8]

Criticisms of the withholding system, while well known for many years, still fall on deaf political ears and an apathetic citizenry. Investopedia provides a comprehensive and accurate list of these criticisms:

1. Taxpayers have no idea how much they pay in taxes and are apathetic about tax rates. If taxpayers had to make one large payment, they would know exactly how much they were forking over for federal taxes, Social Security taxes, Medicare taxes and state taxes. Since the money is taken gradually, many people never pay attention to the full amount, which makes it easier for high tax rates to persist and for the government to increase tax rates.

2. Taxpayer apathy contributes to high levels of government spending. As we all know, the government has a knack for not only spending every single tax dollar it collects, but for running large budget deficits. To continue the previous argument, critics say that when taxpayers don't realize how much of their income is going to the government, they aren't likely to make the connection between their income and the money that is needed to fund new government programs and expand existing ones. Thus, they are likely to support ever-bigger programs without understanding that they're also supporting higher taxes.

3. Taxpayers think that tax refunds are gifts from the government. They don't realize the money was theirs all along and that they've made an interest-free loan to the government all year.

4. Taxpayers treat their refunds as windfalls and don't use the money wisely. A tax refund isn't really a windfall — it's money that you earned that you should have had access to during the year. But when it arrives in a lump sum in the form of a tax refund, it seems like a good excuse to do some extra spending. It's possible to adjust

your withholding so you don't receive a large refund. You can use the extra money in each paycheck to help meet your savings goals throughout the year.

5. Taxpayers can't protest by refusing to pay taxes. Citizens who want to withhold their support for certain types (or all types) of government spending or who believe that the income tax is unconstitutional can have a difficult time keeping their money from the government under the tax withholding system.

6. The system penalizes wage earners. Because taxes aren't withheld from investment income or self-employment income (and a few other less common types of income), the withholding system is said to penalize wage earners, or those whose taxes are collected at the source {from each paycheck}. They have to pay up sooner, which means that their opportunity costs from the withholding system are higher.

7. The system imposes costs on employers. The employers who protested tax withholding in 1913 and got it revoked in 1917 had good points that are still true today. Businesses have to hire additional staff to deal with tax withholding and spend time and money on tax compliance that could be spent on improving their businesses or paying workers more.[8]

This accumulation of evidence culminates in one logical conclusion: we are "pre-paying" our tax bill. Without knowing what our tax liability would be at the end of the year, we are pre-paying via withholding—and because the tax code is so complex, our hope is that we "pre-paid" more than was necessary and, by the grace of the federal government, will receive a tax refund check.

The withholding system allows the progressives to steal the first fruits of your labor and is the initial mechanism cleverly used to impose Marx's second tenet of *The Communist Manifesto*—"a heavy progressive or graduated income tax."[9]

7

★

WHOSE MONEY IS IT?
THE MORALITY OF THE INCOME TAX

"What is so mind boggling is that all of this is being financed by the American people themselves through their own taxes. In other words, the American people are underwriting the destruction of their own freedom and way of life by lavishly financing through federal and state grants the very social scientists who are undermining our national sovereignty and preparing our children to become the dumbed-down vassals of the new world order."

—Samuel L. Blumfield (1927–2015)
American Author, Educator

There is no doubt that the debate over income inequality is about progressivism versus Liberty. When you deploy your individual labor of any kind and, as a result, you earn a dollar, whose dollar is it, anyway? Does it matter if it's wages or profits?

In July 2012, in a Roanoke, Virginia campaign stop, Barack Hussein Obama reached back into the playbook of the Progressive Era during a conversation with Joe the Plumber that became famous.

Per that conversation, he later stated:

There are a lot of wealthy, successful Americans who agree with me—because they want to give something back. They know they didn't—look, if you've been successful, you didn't get there on your own. You didn't get there on your own. I'm always struck by people who think, well, it must be because I was just so smart. There are a lot of smart people out there. It must be because I worked harder than everybody else. Let me tell you something—there are a whole bunch of hardworking people out there.

If you were successful, somebody along the line gave you some help. There was a great teacher somewhere in your life. Somebody helped to create this unbelievable American system that we have that allowed you to thrive. Somebody invested in roads and bridges. If you've got a business—you didn't build that. Somebody else made that happen. The Internet didn't get invented on its own. Government research created the Internet so that all the companies could make money off the Internet.

The point is, is that when we succeed, we succeed because of our individual initiative, but also because we do things together. There are some things, just like fighting fires, we don't do on our own. I mean, imagine if everybody had their own fire service. That would be a hard way to organize fighting fires.[1]

The very next month, liberal U.S. Senator Elizabeth Warren stated at another campaign stop:

I hear all this, you know, "Well, this is class warfare, this is whatever." No. There is nobody in this country who got rich on his own—nobody. You built a factory out there? Good for you. But I want to be clear. You moved your goods to market on the roads the rest of us paid for. You hired workers the rest of us paid to educate. You were safe in your factory because of police forces and fire forces that the rest of us paid for. You didn't have to worry that marauding bands would come and seize everything at your factory—and hire someone to protect against this—because of the work the rest of us did. Now look, you built a factory and it turned into something terrific, or a great idea. God bless—

keep a big hunk of it. But part of the underlying social contract is, you take a hunk of that and pay forward for the next kid who comes along.[2]

Much like the elitists in the Progressive Era, demonizing capitalism, free enterprise, businessmen, businesswomen, entrepreneurs, and industrialists has become a staple of progressives. But, the supposed business-friendly Republicans are not immune. While they may not make such an outrageous statement in public, they continue to support—and even defend—government policies that rob our freedoms through the tax code. Or, they claim adjusting marginal tax rates should somehow be considered "major tax reform."

Columnist Jennifer Rubin responds to Obama's remarks in this *Washington Post* commentary:

> But when he delivered up his "you didn't build that" (whether it was the infrastructure or the small business itself to which he was referring) he revealed a level of resentment toward the private sector that was startling, even to his critics.
>
> Coming right after weeks of Bain [Romney] attacks, his remarks suggested he has issues with wealth creation in general.
>
> He thereby let the anti-business assaults become the campaign. Meanwhile, his affection for government become a chip on his shoulder, prompting him to dare those private-sector wise guys to deny the centrality of government in their success. Yikes.[3]

Steve McCann of the *American Thinker* writes:

> Michael Moore and his fellow-travelers in the American version of the socialist/Marxist cabal have picked up the mantle of defending public unionism in their demonstrations in Madison, Wisconsin and other state capitals. They are vocally calling for more confiscation of the wealth of the rich to pay for the bloated incomes of government workers and openly stating that all wealth

belongs to the state while their true motives are deliberately obfuscated.

The age-old premise and threadbare exhortation of class warfare has long found fertile ground among the lower classes but now they are being mouthed in support of one of the most advantaged groups in America today, public sector workers and their unions.[4]

Progressives subscribe to the ideology that you are not qualified to run your own life or your own affairs and that you should let others—presumptively *smarter* intellectuals than you—manage your money, including determining how much of your income you get to keep. To progressives, government knows best. At the writing of this book, newly elected Congresswoman Alexandria Ocasio-Cortez defended her stance for a 70 percent tax rate on the *rich*. For progressives, the socialist mantra never changes throughout history. Your money is theirs, and they think they can spend it more effectively than you!

When Obama and other progressive socialists claim that a successful entrepreneur used the highways, roads, and infrastructure to create their wealth, he fails to recognize that the entrepreneur paid for them, too, and more than likely contributed *more* to the establishment and upkeep of the infrastructure than the regular wage earner. If a successful entrepreneur has higher income, a state that has state income tax will likely require he or she to pay more of their earnings to support state infrastructures (progressive rate structure). If that entrepreneur bought a half-million-dollar Rolls Royce, his or her sales tax contribution to the state is much greater than if he or she had purchased at $30,000 Chevrolet. That V-12 Rolls Royce that gets twelve miles to the gallon uses more fuel, too; therefore, the owner pays more in state and federal gasoline excise taxes. The examples are endless. See where this is going?

To say the wealthy class of society doesn't "pay their fair share" is comical on its face. When a socialist like Ocasio-Cortez makes this type of statement, it is a progressive dog whistle, stating that upper-income folks need to be penalized for their success and their largesse needs to be redistributed.

What social justice progressives choose to ignore is that we all have access to the same infrastructure. Why is it some are wildly successful, and some are not? Of course, luck can be involved but, typically, one's choices in life are more of a determining factor in one's ultimate success than the use of Route 66.

Most intellectual arguments on the theory of progressive taxation are fundamentally based on the Marxist dogma of one's "ability to pay." But, progressives have taken this context a giant step forward with the grand design elements of social justice.

Does someone who earns $500,000 per year receive more value in using the nearest U.S. highway than someone making $25,000 per year? Should the higher-earning American pay more for the use of that highway than the lower-earning individual?

The major flaw of progressive redistribution is its theoretical basis, similar to communism, that everyone is equal—*equal in work ethic, equal in aptitude, equal in education, and equal in their choice of occupation.* Therefore, according to the socialists, an individual who may work harder or longer, chooses to be more educated, starts a business, or chooses a higher-paying occupation becomes "unequal," and is, therefore, more responsible for a greater share of the cost of government.

Elitist socialist intellectuals argue that since the infrastructure value of higher earners is greater, they should pay a disproportionate share of the cost of that infrastructure, military defense, and welfare. According to them, they simply have more to lose and have benefited from government greater than lower-income individuals.

Alternative tax structures are commonly labeled as "regressive," which means as the overall tax burden is more unequally distributed, the lower incomes pay a higher share of the tax burden and, thus, a disproportionate percentage of their income. For this reason, innovative alternative tax solutions such as a true flat tax or a consumption tax (similar to the FairTax) are roundly criticized by the socialists.

Based on the intent of our Founders, the fairest tax system devised is the per capita (or head) tax. This is where the cost of government is divided equally among each citizen according to the census. This, of course, is the most transparent and equitable form of taxation. Yet, because it is so transparent, modern-day politicians would never want you to see the true cost of government in the form an annual tax bill sent to each citizen. The Founders had always intended for taxes to be apportioned this way, which is why, in 1895, the income tax was ruled unconstitutional because it was a direct tax and not apportioned.

Assigning increased tax liability to one citizen at a higher rate than another is simply an unfair scheme to engineer specific social outcomes and flies in the face of *securing the blessings* for all promised in our Constitution. The Constitution does not delineate *the general Welfare* or the equal *Blessings of Liberty* based on your level of income.

The U.S. Constitution states in the Preamble:

> *We the People of the United States, in Order to form a more perfect Union, establish Justice, insure domestic Tranquility, provide for the common defense, promote the general Welfare, and secure the Blessings of Liberty to ourselves and our Posterity, do ordain and establish this Constitution for the United States of America.*

Our Founders also did not state certain unalienable "Rights of Life, Liberty and pursuit of Happiness" vary among taxable income brackets.

The Declaration of Independence states: "We hold these truths to be self-evident, that all men are created equal, that they are endowed by their Creator with certain unalienable Rights, that among these are Life, Liberty and the pursuit of Happiness."

America is a Constitutional Representative Republic; yet, we have devised a morally corrupt government revenue scheme that is completely undemocratic in its application. It can be morally argued that if one's liability to fund the expense of government is progressively assigned to those at higher income brackets, then those people who are bearing the majority burden of the cost of government should have more weighted impact assigned to their votes. For example, if you were to pay the top personal income tax rate at the writing of this book at 38 percent, then should your vote count more than someone who pays nothing at all? Should it count more than someone, say, at the 15-percent income tax bracket?

In America, all citizens have the right to opportunity. Progressives argue that those in the minority, low income or specific classes, have less opportunity than most. In those instances, we should, in fact, be providing opportunities for less fortunate citizens to realize the American Dream. But, it is completely un-American and against our Founders' intent that we forcibly take from one group and redistribute to another. It would be a short debate indeed for someone to argue that the simple act of progressively taxing one group creates opportunity for another.

By virtue of withholding of wages, the average American has no way to protest taxes in the same way our Founders did — by refusing to pay taxes on tea to the British crown.

Our federal government today uses public funds acquired from our taxes to spend in ways inconceivable and unimaginable to those gathered at the Constitutional Convention. Gone is the adherence to the limitations of a federal government to its narrow list of enumerated powers.

Citizens are forced to endure a forcible tax and enforcement structure that may send funds to objectionable causes. Does the government infringe on someone's First Amendment right to Freedom of Religion, for example, when a Christian opposes the funding of abortion factories at Planned Parenthood? Do they have the right to directly withhold that portion of our taxes that fund an ideal that goes against our religious beliefs, thus usurping our First Amendment right to Freedom of Religion?

What about funds that are sent to countries that have ideologies we oppose? What about sending taxpayer funds to countries that hate us or ones we consider an enemy or proponent of terrorism, such as the $400 million (in cash no less) sent to Iran by the Obama administration?[5]

Citizen taxpayers aren't allowed to designate or earmark their tax contributions; therefore, if you were a conscientious objector, objecting to funding government-paid abortions or to giving American taxpayer cash to a foreign enemy or a foreign government that does not respect human rights, you're out of luck. Since 2009, the United States government has given away almost $221 billion to foreign countries. You may wonder why, or for what purposes, our tax dollars are given to the following countries as recently as 2018:

- Jordan $816.1 Million
- Ethiopia $803.8 Million
- South Sudan $740.1 Million
- Sudan $740.1 Million
- Syria $633.8 Million
- Kenya $591.5 Million
- Yemen $448.7 Million
- Somalia $421.6 Million
- Iraq $384.9 Million
- South Africa $355.4 Million
- Haiti $262.5 Million
- Indonesia $245.3 Million
- West Bank/Gaza $200.1 Million
- Colombia $181.8 Million
- Guatemala $163.1 Million
- Egypt $143.2 Million
- Honduras $124.1 Million
- El Salvador $94.7 Million
- Mexico $51.9 Million
- Libya $45.4 Million
- Nicaragua $33.4 Million
- China $11.5 Million
- Venezuela $6.7 Million

*Source: ForeignAssistance.gov[6]

Does that list and do those amounts raise any eyebrows? Notwithstanding any argument about whether the Constitution permits this type of distribution of taxpayers' funds; what about the larger morality question? For instance, there are several countries on that list that are primarily Muslim. They do not grant women the same rights as men and punish homosexuals and adulterers with state-sponsored death penalties. Do you approve of a percentage of your taxes going to those regimes?

How about China? They're our most fierce competitor on the world's economic stage; why would the U.S. give them $11 million?

We have streams of migrant caravans coming from Central America; yet, nearly $500 million in aid was poured into that region in 2018 — and the caravans keep coming. How do you feel about the staggering amounts going to African countries, where some of the most corrupt regimes in the world reside? Are these huge foreign-aid payments to African countries designed to be some sort of backhanded reparations for slavery?

The U.S. gives foreign aid to countries that are known to harbor terrorists and who do little to assist the United States in their capture. Countries like Yemen and Sudan are swimming in foreign aid known as *your* tax dollars.

Consider the welfare state. America rose to the greatest country in the world based on its citizens' incredible civic intellect, rugged individualism, and stubborn self-reliance. Those who were down and out or needed a hand-up were generally helped by neighbors and their church congregations. There was no need for a welfare state. Today, the food stamp and welfare rolls (52 million as of 2015)[7] are larger than America's total population (50.1 million)[8] from the last census before the Progressive Era began (1880) in the United States. These latest welfare numbers for which data was available only included "means-tested" benefits and did not include Social Security or veterans' benefits. Over 21 percent of our population was receiving benefits such as WIC, housing assistance, Medicaid, etc.

According to the Cato Institute, over $1 trillion in wealth redistribution was direct payments to this class of recipients in 2015. This massive transfer of wealth has led to 21 percent of our population participating in some type of welfare.[9]

Gone is that famous American self-reliance, ousted by the confiscatory progressive tax system that was designed to cure poverty but has only increased dependency on the bottomless checkbook of our current tax revenue system.

The vast majority of Americans are generous to a fault and take great measures to help the less fortunate, but the progressives have robbed us of the ability to direct our generosity at a local level, specifically, where our morals, values, and ethics believe these efforts should be deposited. In the proven theory that government doesn't do many tasks very well, the welfare system is the Holy Grail of government ineptitude. For those of us that believe in a hand-up instead of a handout, our money is being robbed and redistributed as the bureaucrats and Congress think is feasible, many times littered with corruption, graft, and incompetence. The income tax has allowed politicians to effectively exchange handouts for votes, increasing welfare exponentially.

Today, the progressives are likely to tout studies showing growing income inequality in America, which, to them, justify making the marginal tax rates even more progressive and punitive.

But don't believe them. According to "Five Myths about Economic Inequality in America," a 2016 policy research paper by Michael Tanner of the Cato Institute, the income inequality arguments are technically and factually flawed:

> Overall, the rich get rich because they work for it. And they work hard. For example, research by economists Mark Aguiar of the Federal Reserve Bank of Boston and Erik Hurst of the University of Chicago found that the working time for upper-income professionals has increased since 1965, while working time for low-skill, low-income workers has decreased. [10]

Today, similar to the Progressive Era wherein elitist intellectuals consistently claimed the "evil" rich got that way on the backs of the poor and labor class, Tanner offers this:

> There is little demonstrable relationship between inequality and poverty. Poverty rates have sometimes risen during periods of relatively stable levels of inequality and declined during times of rising inequality. The idea that gains by one person necessarily mean losses by another reflects a zero-sum view of the economy that is simply untethered to

history or economics. The economy is not fixed in size, with the only question being one of distribution. Rather, the entire pie can grow, with more resources available to all.... In the popular imagination, it is an unrestrained free market that gives rise to inequality, and a powerful government is necessary to act as a counterweight. In reality, big government is often complicit with, and frequently the cause of, inequality.[10]

Despite the progressives' unrelenting logic that free-market capitalism drives income inequality, Tanner's data extinguishes this myth.

Tanner does go on to state how big business cronyism can lead to disparities in income, but these are isolated cases and represent a small or tiny percentage of the overall market. To further destroy the myth that a redistributive progressive tax code is necessary to reduce income inequality, Tanner smartly and succinctly concludes:

Of course, even if one accepts the premise that inequality is increasing, undeserved, and leads to the problems discussed above, the more interesting question from a policy perspective is what we can — or should — do about it. There are, after all, two ways to reduce inequality. One can attempt to bring the bottom up by reducing poverty, or one can bring the top down by, in effect, punishing the rich.

Traditionally, we have tried to reduce inequality by taxing the rich and redistributing that money to the poor. And, as noted above, we have achieved some success. But we may well have reached a point of diminishing returns from such policies. Despite the United States spending roughly a trillion dollars each year on antipoverty programs at all levels of government, by the official poverty measure we have done little to reduce poverty. Even by using more accurate alternative poverty measures, gains leveled out during the 1970s, apart from the latter part of the 1990s when the booming economy and the reform of the welfare system produced significant reductions in poverty. Additional increases in spending have yielded few gains.

Thus, while redistribution may have reduced overall inequality, it has done far less to help lift people out of poverty.

And even in terms of attacking inequality, redistribution may have reached the limits of its ability to make a difference. A new study from the Brookings Institution, for example, suggests that further increasing taxes on the wealthy, accompanied by increased transfers to the poor, would have relatively little effect on inequality. This study by William Gale, Melissa Kearney, and Peter Orszag looked at what outcome could be expected if the top tax rate was raised to 50 percent from its current 39.6 percent, and all additional revenue raised was redistributed to households in the lowest quintile of current incomes. To bias the study in favor of redistribution, the authors assume no change in behavior from the wealthy in an effort to reduce their exposure to the higher tax rate. The tax hike, therefore, would raise $96 billion in additional revenue, which would allow additional "Economic growth, after all, depends on people who are ambitious, skilled risk-takers." redistribution of $2,650 to each household in the bottom quintile—an amount that would not significantly reduce inequality. The authors conclude, "That such a sizable increase in the top personal income tax rate leads to a strikingly limited reduction in income inequality speaks to the limitations of this particular approach to addressing the broader challenge."

Indeed, many advocates of increased taxes for the wealthy seem to concede that their efforts would do little to reduce poverty. Rather, they would reduce inequality from the top down. Piketty, for example, argues for a globally imposed wealth tax and a U.S. income tax rate of 80 percent on incomes over $500,000 per year. He acknowledges this tax "would not bring the government much in the way of revenue," but that it would "distribute the fruits of growth more widely while imposing reasonable limits on economically useless (or even harmful) behavior."

Other critics of inequality seem equally concerned with punishing the rich. Hillary Clinton, for instance, argues that fighting inequality requires a "toppling" of the one percent. But the ultimate losers of such policies are likely to be the poor. Piketty's plan might indeed lead to a society that would be more equal, but it would also likely be a society where everyone is far poorer.

Economic growth, after all, depends on people who are ambitious, skilled risk-takers. We need such people to be ever-striving for more in order to fuel economic growth. That means they must be rewarded for their efforts, their skills, their ambitions, and their risks. Such rewards inevitably lead to greater inequality. But as Nobel Economics Prize-winning economist Gary Becker pointed out, "It would be hard to motivate the vast majority of individuals to exert much effort, including creative effort, if everyone had the same earnings, status, prestige, and other types of rewards."

To be sure, since the 1970s the relationship between economic growth and poverty reduction has been uneven at best. But we are unlikely to see significant reductions in poverty without strong economic growth. Punishing the segment of society that most contributes to such growth therefore seems a poor policy for serious poverty reduction.

But one needn't be a fan of the Laffer curve to realize that raising taxes on the rich can have unforeseen consequences. Recall 19th century French economist and classical liberal Frédéric Bastiat's "What Is Seen and What Is Not Seen," which argues that the pernicious effects of government policies are not easily identified because they affect incentives and thus people's willingness to work and take risks. And recall that money earned by the rich is either saved or spent. If saved, it provides a pool of capital that fuels investment and provides jobs to the non-rich. Likewise, if spent, it increases consumption, similarly providing increased employment opportunities for the non-rich.

Back in 1991, for example, Congress decided to impose a luxury tax on such frivolous items as high-priced automobiles, aircraft, jewelry, furs, and yachts. The tax "worked" in a sense: the rich bought fewer luxury goods — and thousands of Americans who worked in the jewelry, aircraft, and boating industries lost their jobs. According to a study done for the Joint Economic Committee, the tax destroyed 7,600 jobs in the boating industry alone. Most of the tax was soon repealed, although the luxury tax provision lasted until 2002.

Too much of the debate over economic inequality has been driven by emotion or misinformation. Yes, there is a significant amount of inequality in America, but most estimates of that inequality fail to account for the amount of redistribution that already takes place in our system. If one takes into account taxes and social welfare programs, the gap between rich and poor shrinks significantly. Inequality does not disappear after making these adjustments, but it may not be as big a problem or be growing as rapidly as is sometimes portrayed.

But even if inequality were as bad as advertised, one has to ask why that should be considered a problem. Of course, inequality may be a problem if the wealthy became rich through unfair means. But, in reality, most wealthy people earned their wealth, and did so by providing goods and services that benefit society as "Policies designed to reduce inequality by imposing new burdens on the wealthy may perversely harm the poor." Moreover, there remains substantial economic mobility in American society, although as noted above, there are policy reforms often unmentioned in the inequality debate that could expand the opportunities available to people toward the bottom of the income distribution, such as education reform, reducing occupational licensing and other regulatory barriers to entrepreneurship, reforming the criminal justice system, and eliminating the perverse incentives of the welfare system. Those who are rich today may not remain rich tomorrow. And those who are poor may still rise out of poverty.

While inequality per se may not be a problem, poverty is. But there is little evidence to suggest that economic inequality increases poverty. Indeed, policies designed to reduce inequality by imposing new burdens on the wealthy may perversely harm the poor by slowing economic growth and reducing job opportunities.[10]

Inevitably, progressives argue that a progressive income tax system is moral and, therefore, needed to curb poverty. The productive class in our society are increasingly asked to shoulder the burden of the rest of America. Cato Institute's John F. Early states this in his 2018 policy analysis paper entitled, "Reassessing the Facts about Inequality, Poverty and Redistribution":

A report from the Congressional Budget Office estimates that the top 1 percent paid 25.4 percent of all federal taxes in 2013, compared to 15 percent of pre-tax income. The wealthy pay a disproportionate amount of taxes. At the same time, lower-income earners benefit disproportionately from a variety of wealth transfer programs. The federal government alone, for example, currently funds more than 100 anti-poverty programs, dozens of which provide either cash or in-kind benefits directly to individuals. Federal spending on those programs approached $700 billion in 2015, and state and local governments added another $300 billion. . . . Most families that are defined as "poor" have many goods and services that would be classified as luxury items. Air conditioning is seven times more prevalent among poor families today than among the general population when the War on Poverty began. Most poor families have microwave ovens, at least one vehicle, video games, flat-screen TVs, and personal computers.[9]

[In a stunning conclusion, this report surmises:]

More than 50 years after the United States declared the War on Poverty, poverty is almost entirely gone.

Independent data show that families classified as poor have lifestyles that would usually be considered middle class. Government spends more $1 trillion annually in the name of reducing poverty.

Yet the measurement system continues to report no reduction in poverty, and substantial taxpayer dollars go to people who are not poor. The public has also been misled by similar false signals about income inequality. The official estimates are deficient on several dimensions and exaggerate the degree of income inequality. Public policy debate should begin with the realization that only about 2 percent of the population—not 13.5 percent—live in poverty.

Government annually takes more than $1 trillion from above-average earners and gives it to low earners so that all except a small fraction receive middle-income status. As a result, income inequality in America is not significantly different from that of other advanced nations. The policy debate now has a firm quantitative foundation for evaluating whether more spending or less spending on poverty and income equality is desirable and how that spending should be structured. Additional analysis can explore the ethical, efficacy, efficiency, and overall economic health dimensions of inequality and poverty policy in the context of more accurate estimates of the underlying economic measures.[9]

Government spending is an outward expression of what priorities have been established by both parties. There is a moral argument for taxes, and the Constitution calls for apportioned taxes in specific, enumerated powers.

There simply is no credible moral argument for a graduated progressive income for purposes of correcting the progressives' imagined income inequalities—or to fight the war on poverty. Instead, it has become more obvious than ever that a progressive graduated income tax is, in effect, immoral.

A later chapter is devoted to the morality of the transfer payments made to illegal aliens via the welfare system embedded in the progressive income tax code. In March 2019, the *Washington Examiner* reported that a 2014 analysis proves 63 percent of non-citizens are using "cash" welfare, which includes the earned income tax credit (EITC). [11]

This was compared to only 35 percent of citizen households. The report stated there are nearly 4.7 million non-citizen households currently receiving welfare. [11]

What, specifically, is the moral argument for taking money out the pockets of hardworking American citizens to make direct cash payments to illegal non-citizens, who don't pay any federal income taxes? And this report is from five years ago before we started seeing the huge migrant caravans that are amassing at our southern border! How many are on welfare today?

Consider another element of this draconian system of taxation on moral grounds. The burden of compliance with the juggernaut that is the tax code is so grueling, few citizens can file their annual income tax returns without assistance.

Most Americans have not been audited by the IRS, but the specter of Big Brother looking over their shoulder and the threat of seizures, garnishments, and audits looms over every taxpayer.

A fiercely liberty-minded group of colonists, by which this country was founded, could never have imagined in their worst nightmares a government with direct taxing authority — it's not just immoral, it's downright abusive.

In his piece in the *Washington Times*, Richard W. Rahn provides real clarity on the immorality of the IRS and the income tax and their methods of terrorizing the citizenry. Regarding income tax and the IRS, Rahn describes the loss of Liberty in just a partial list of the abuses that are fostered by this type of progressive taxation by the agency that wields the absolute power to destroy lives:

- Unnecessarily strikes fear into the hearts of tens of millions of your fellow citizens, causing such anguish and despair that some are driven to suicide each year.
- Requires citizens to know 10 million words of rules and regulations because the failure to do so may result in

draconian fines and even jail, while at the same time no one in the agency has a full understanding of all the rules and regulations it requires others to know.

- Routinely ignores the constitutional protections against self-incrimination and the right to the presumption of innocence.
- Seizes the assets of citizens without obtaining court judgments.
- Penalizes marriage.
- Discriminates against many of the nation's most productive citizens.
- Destroys incentives to work, save and invest, and undermines job creation.
- Routinely protects agency personnel who have engaged in citizen intimidation, misrepresentation or worse?
- No, I am not referring to the Nazi SS or the Soviet KGB, but the IRS, which is guilty of all of the above and more.[12]

It is, of course, true that no one loves the tax collector and that taxes are the price we pay for a civil society. But, as with anything else, there are proper and improper taxes and tax collection procedures and methods. According to news accounts, attacks and threats against IRS personnel are rising, and unfortunately, this trend is likely to continue until there is a fundamental change in our tax laws and collection methods. People who do not have access to the media and cannot afford expensive tax lawyers sometimes reach such a level of frustration with the IRS that they resort to violent or irrational behavior. IRS officials and workers will say the tax code is not their fault—it is the fault of Congress—and they are only doing their jobs.

It is unambiguously true that the tax code and IRS are creatures of Congress, with all of its self-dealing, corruption, ignorance, and incompetence. But it also is true, and was made explicit at the Nuremberg trials, that those who carry out orders that they know to be wrong or should know to be wrong are not absolved of personal responsibility.

The county tax collector who is responsible for the collection of property taxes is engaged in a necessary activity because it is through his or her efforts that the local police, fire departments, and schools are funded. In most places, all pay the same tax rate, with those having more expensive properties paying proportionally more and vice versa. The tax, and how it is applied, is readily understood by most people. Even though many may complain about the tax rate, the tax itself is generally considered fair.

Similarly, those who work in a state sales-tax collection office are administering a tax whose proceeds go for purposes that are generally understood—schools, roads, parks, etc. The tax itself is nondiscriminatory and is easy to comprehend. As a result, there tends to be little general hostility against property- and sales-tax collectors, most people viewing their job as a necessary function.

Unlike the local property and sales taxes, the federal income tax and the IRS have perverted the law, which is supposed to ensure equal justice, into an instrument of plunder through legislation (as contrasted with constitutional law) and regulation. The Constitution gives the federal government the right to tax for the "common Defense" and "general [not specific] welfare" (e.g., the Centers for Disease Control and Prevention). Many of the current departments of government (e.g., the Departments of Housing, Energy, Education, and Health and Human Services) seem to have no constitutional basis, and nowhere does the Constitution give the federal government the power to engage in income redistribution.

Most of the Founding Fathers were students of the Scottish Enlightenment, and the most influential book on their thinking was Adam Smith's *The Wealth of Nations*, published in 1776. (Smith and Ben Franklin were personal friends.) In his section on taxation, Smith said: "The subjects of every state ought to contribute towards the support of the government…that is, in proportion to the revenue which they respectively enjoy under the protection of the state." In modern parlance, Smith was endorsing a proportional or "flat tax," or VAT, or sales tax. Smith went on to say, "The tax which each individual is bound to pay ought to be certain, and not arbitrary. Where it is otherwise, every person subject to the tax is put more or less in the power of the tax gatherer…." Finally, Smith noted: "Every tax ought to be so contrived as both to take out and to keep out of the pockets of the people as little as possible, over and above what it brings into the public treasury of the state." The income tax and IRS fail on all accounts, and neither Smith nor the American Founders would have approved. [13]

The French political and economic philosopher Frédéric Bastiat correctly said "No society can exist unless the laws are respected to a certain degree, but the safest way to make them respected is to make them respectable. When law and morality are in contradiction to each other, the citizen finds himself in the cruel alternative of either losing his moral sense, or of losing his respect for the law." The tax law could be made fair, certain and efficient. The tragedy is that too many at the IRS and in Congress have lost their moral sense, causing their fellow citizens to lose respect for the law.[13]

A simple morality argument can be made for the pain, suffering, and costs inflicted on a taxpayer that simply tries to comply with a 77,000-page tax code that has nearly four million words. According to Senator Ted Cruz, the tax code has more words than the Holy Bible. PolitiFact confirms the Senator's statement:

A 2010 report by the Internal Revenue Service's Taxpayer's Advocate Office found that the tax code contained 3.8 million words. That calculation was made by downloading a zipped file of the code, unzipping it and running it through Microsoft Word's word count feature, according to a footnote in the report. A 2012 version of the report puts the number of words in the code at "about 4 million." We also reached out to CCH, the Riverwoods, Ill.-based publisher of the two-volume 2013 Winter version of the tax code and was told the best estimate of word length was 4 million. That was two years ago, but we think it's a safe bet that the length of the tax code has only increased since then, not decreased.[14]

Dennis Olson, the Charles T. Haley Professor of Old Testament Theology at the Princeton Theological Seminary, told *PolitiFact New Jersey* that a fair approximation of the Bible's length is 800,000 words for the Old and New Testaments combined. "The King James Version would be 823,156 while the more recent New Revised Standard Version would be 774,746 words."

Hellen Mardaga, an assistant professor of New Testament at Catholic University in Washington, agreed that estimates that put the Bible at 800,000 words were credible. Put it all together and the tax code is roughly five times as long as the Bible. So, Cruz is correct.

The immoral politicians and bureaucrats from both major parties use the income tax as their personal playground to harvest votes, reward lobbyists, and punish enemies, as well as to achieve the Marxist ideology of social engineering via the tax code.

There are huge sums of money to be made by connected politicians and lobbyists in the design and administration of the tax code. At a minimum, favors to change the tax code for a large political donor can help a politician win an endorsement from a significant member of the donor class, whether it is from a government union boss or a multibillionaire industrialist. Many times, these cozy relationships are at the expense of America's well-being as a whole—and are completely and blatantly immoral.

A research paper produced by the Mercatus Center at George Mason University reports:

> The structure of individual and corporate income taxes in the United States—accounting for over 55 percent of total tax revenue—reflects policymakers' agglomerated attempts to increase fairness, conduct social policy, encourage

economic growth, and promote favored industries. According to the National Taxpayer Advocate, between 2001 and 2010 there were 4,428 changes to the Internal Revenue Code, including an estimated 579 changes in 2010 alone. To put this in perspective, it means the tax code averages more than one change per day. The complexity of tax code is largely responsible for the $67 billion to $378 billion of accounting costs incurred in the process of filing taxes. A simpler tax system with fewer deductions would assist in alleviating these costs.

Revenue collected by the government through taxes prevents economic transactions from occurring. The economic size of these purchases and business deals that do not occur is larger than the revenues collected by the government.

Along with accounting costs and economic costs, lobbying costs are the third cost of today's tax code. Although we do not have an estimate of annual lobbying costs, between 2002 and 2011 lobbyists spent $27.6 billion petitioning federal, state, and local governments for policy preferences. More significantly for long-term economic growth, a tax code open to lobbyists incentivizes the pursuit of rent-seeking careers, rather than innovation, to protect and expand tax advantages.[15]

It is morally reprehensible that America, borne by the blood of patriots, requires its citizens to comply and absorb the costs associated with a massive Marxist ideology that is purposely designed and fomented to confuse the masses and create a compliance structure that is neither fair nor transparent.

Within a tax system like that of the United States, which is primarily enforced through voluntary compliance, it remains the taxpayer's obligation to compute and submit taxes to the IRS. This voluntary tax compliance is achieved through hours of taxpayer efforts and through hired tax consultants. The accounting costs of complying with the tax code range from $67 billion to $378 billion. About 60 percent of individual taxpayers and 71 percent of unincorporated business taxpayers pay someone else (i.e., an accountant, lawyer, or tax professional) to prepare their taxes. An additional 32 percent of individual taxpayers use tax preparation software. As a direct result of the large and growing complexity in the income tax code, the vast majority of Americans now incur some type of expense to determine their income tax liability and comply with filing requirements.[15]

And, finally, how morally reprehensible is it that 44 percent of income tax filers pay nothing at all? Regardless of the nightly drumbeat by pundits on liberal media about how the so-called rich should pay their fair share, how about requiring the 44 percent that pay nothing to pay something?

The United States was founded as a Constitutional Representative Republic. But, what if we taxpayers could earmark our personal tax dollars to the programs that we believe are the most worthwhile? How novel would that be? How badly would Congress scream at their loss of power and graft from lobbyists?

Suppose you could fill out a form and designate how your next year's taxes would be spent. If you paid $10,000 in taxes for the year, you could designate 20 percent to defense, 10 percent to retire the debt, 70 percent to other causes — and purposely not designate any dollars to Planned Parenthood or foreign aid to Yemen or Sudan or Indonesia. Of course, some would argue that national defense would get underfunded this way and that percentage would have to be locked down. What about welfare? How much would you designate to those that don't work? Would you continue to authorize your tax dollars for earned income tax credits to illegal aliens whose dependents aren't even in the country?

Even if your conscious screams at the morality of the way in which your tax dollars are spent and whom they are spent on, you have no Liberty in choosing the use of those tax dollars. Try being a conscientious objector when it comes to holding back your tax payments in protest. Dr. Martin Luther King, Jr. stated that "noncooperation with evil is as much a moral obligation as is cooperation with good." Yet, the IRS doesn't recognize this form of civil disobedience and a tax objector on grounds of conscious would be subject to civil and criminal penalties. In the *United States v. Lee* (1982), the Supreme Court ruled: "The tax system could not function if denominations were allowed to challenge the tax system because tax payments were spent in a manner that violates their religious beliefs."[16]

There go your First Amendment rights....

As of the writing of this chapter, the National Debt Clock showed the U.S. national debt at over $22 trillion—or $180,170 per taxpayer.[17] Some may believe there is a moral case to be made to earmark some of your taxes to retire the debt and to not leave your children or grandchildren with the growing, monstrous burden. The government will happily let you know that you can make extra payments to the Treasury for this purpose, but you can't specifically designate a portion of taxes due as you see fit.

We have not held our elected representatives accountable. We have a history of progressive congresses and occupants of the White House that have apparently known better than American citizens (up to and including you and I) how tax revenue should be collected—and how and what it should be spent on.

Imagine spending your lifetime building assets to pass down to your children and grandchildren, but your heirs are left to sell the assets you passed down, like a farm, ranch, or business just to pay the estate taxes. The socialists believe those assets belong to the collective.

The death tax or estate tax is one of the more insidious outgrowths of progressivism. Like the original income tax, this tax was also meant to soak the very rich. During the Progressive Era, this tax was used in newspaper media cartoons to portray trust babies sitting idly by while the rest of the nation toiled in low-paying, industrial jobs. The socialists argue that having an estate tax is another form of social justice, preventing the concentration of wealth in the hands of a few over generations.

Socialists reason that their support for the estate tax is the concept of equal opportunity as a basis for the social contract, or the legitimacy of the state over the individual. An estate tax is a double-tax by any standard. When a citizen earns wages or profits in the progressive tax system we have today, he or she has already paid income taxes and/or capital gains taxes on investment income. For the government to come and tax another huge bite out of what the citizen has built is completely immoral.

Currently, there are fifteen states in the U.S. that also have an inheritance tax or estate tax in addition to the tax at the federal level. Governments love to stick their fingers in the cookie jar that you and I have spent a lifetime building. It's difficult to imagine, but the reality is the government gets the very first fruits of your labor— even before your children and grandchildren.

The IRS has reported that their estate lawyers were the most productive attorneys at the agency, finding $2,200 of taxes that people owe the government for each hour they work.[18] Imagine dealing with settling an estate when a family member passes, then having these vultures waiting to audit the estate?

> *"John Doe was a salt of the earth man. You know, the kind of man you could meet at the local diner and truly enjoy talking with. He farmed all his life on property handed down to him by his father and from his father before him. At his death, Mr. Doe was 86 years old and owned 500 acres of land. His real estate alone was worth $2.5 million. John had one son, Jack, to whom he left his farm. As with many farmers, his wealth was primarily in his land. Without the land, there would be no farm, without the farm, John could not have provided for his family. John paid real estate taxes on the farm for years. His ancestors paid taxes on the real estate long before him. John was always a productive member of his community. In fact, many people swore the milk he produced was the best around. John never asked for and never received government handouts."*

If John had died in 2012, there would have been no federal estate tax paid on the transfer of the property to Jack. However, John died after January 1, 2013, only $1 million of the $2.5 million is exempt from taxes, with the remaining $1.5 million being taxed at the new rate of 55%, resulting in a tax bill of $825,000.00 for the federal government. Jack, as the executor of his father's estate, is forced to sell at least 165 acres of his family farm to pay the tax bill to the government.[19]

Try to find the morality in this family having to sell 33 percent of their family farm to "redistribute" wealth according to the socialist creed? Even though the latest Trump tax cuts increased the exemption, why do we still have a death tax whatsoever?

America has allowed its politicians and bureaucrats to impose immoral, progressive, punitive, and socialistic income and death taxes incrementally until it's become an unfortunate but accepted way of American life.

8

★

PATRIOTISM & PAYING TAXES

"By today's standards King George III was a very mild tyrant indeed. He taxed his American colonists at a rate of only pennies per annum. His actual impact on their personal lives was trivial. He had arbitrary power over them in law and in principle but in fact it was seldom exercised. If you compare his rule with that of today's U.S. Government you have to wonder why we celebrate our independence."

—Joseph Sobran (1946–2010)
Conservative Review Syndicated Columnist

Throughout the research, I continually discovered progressive quotes, columns, and opinion pieces on how "patriotic" it was to pay taxes.

The common theme of these diatribes was that paying taxes should make you feel *patriotic* and that everyone should strive to pay *more* in taxes.

Prior to the American Revolution, the colonists were incensed over tax policies imposed by the British crown and parliament. The Stamp Act, the Sugar Act, the Townsend Act and other various directives on the colonies without direct representation in parliament drove the colonists to develop a fierce anti-tax legacy that has prevailed in America's consciousness for one hundred and thirty-seven years until 1913, and to some lesser extent since. As noted in a previous chapter, this period of non-direct taxation policies, which were established in the Constitution, brought America an unrivaled economy, prosperity, and freedom.

The most common government use of patriotism to justify taxation is during brief periods of war, such as the War of 1812, where excise taxes and import tariffs were raised to pay for it.

The Bandy Heritage Center states:

When war finally looked inevitable, the Secretary of the Treasury, Albert Gallatin, submitted his financial plan; he believed existing revenue sufficient to cover regular government expenses, but the costs of the war required borrowing $10 million just for 1812. Fiscally conservative, many Congressmen recoiled at his proposal, but most signed off on Gallatin's proposals by March. Congress approved a loan of $11 million and higher customs duties to cover military expenditures. Under no circumstances would Congress approve new internal taxes in 1812.[1]

But, even during a crisis, America was not inclined to approve new internal taxes unless absolutely necessary.

Lincoln goaded Congress into passing an unconstitutional income tax to fund the Union in the Civil War. Why wasn't this challenged before it was finally allowed to expire in 1873? Because nobody in Congress was willing to be publicly *unpatriotic* and challenge the effort needed to win the war and, ultimately, to pay the debts caused by the war.

This scenario is seen once again with calls for the income tax during the Spanish-American War, even though it was the shortest war in our history (slightly over three months). Progressives have always subscribed to the theory of allowing no calamity to go waste, no matter how small, without projecting their taxing agenda.

Discussing new taxes required by the federal government prior to World War II, IRS historian Shelly L. Davis notes:

The Internal Revenue Bureau (predecessor to the IRS) launched a special public education program to help citizens understand the new tax burden. A nationwide campaign of education and publicity was organized. A special effort was made to popularize the war taxes by emphasizing the needs of the country and appealing to national pride and patriotism.

The war created popular acceptance of the income tax by making the paying of it a patriotic duty. Government speakers known as "Four-Minute Men" fanned out across the nation, preaching about the importance of "defeating the Hun" by paying taxes promptly and fully.[2]

Pravda and the Politburo couldn't have created a more effective propaganda scheme to coerce Americans to happily and willfully agree to pay more taxes.

All the while, as we have seen throughout American history, wars are convenient excuses to soak its citizenry and continue to use the tax code to orchestrate progressive social change.

Teddy Roosevelt made it vogue for Americans to demand his and the progressives' determination of what is the *fair* distribution of tax responsibility, which, throughout history, has translated to mean a progressive income tax. Somehow, America's staunch individualism was slowly being replaced by class warfare, income equality, and identity politics.

Surely, the increase in the progressive rates and tax brackets that were invoked during World War I would only be temporary to pay for the war? They weren't. The income tax began as a flat tax on the richest Americans. Now that Congress had the vehicle to turn on the revenue faucet at will, no war would ever seem too costly to enter.

When the income tax brackets were increased to pay for World War I, they never went back.

In June 1940, before Pearl Harbor, Davis further notes how Congress seized an opportunity to fill the federal coffers in anticipation of entering into World War II.

The Revenue Act of 1940 raised the debt limit to $4 Billion in order to authorize the issuance of defense bonds. This act increased federal surtaxes on most individual income tax brackets by imposing a defense supertax of 10 percent on most existing internal revenue taxes. Personal exemptions were reduced by 60 percent and corporate tax rates increased only slightly in anticipation of new excess profits tax.

This act also raised excise taxes on distilled spirits, wines, cigarettes, and playing cards. This act implemented the use of the gross rather than net income to determine the need to file an income tax return. This act increased tax rates on corporations, individual surtax rates, and nonresident aliens. This act imposed a flat tax of 10 percent of the tax computed, designated as a "Defense Tax" effective for a five-year period.[2]

Did Congress know something the American people didn't six months before Pearl Harbor? Could this "*Defense Tax,*" passed in advance for a five-year period, suggest that was how long they anticipated the war would last? Isn't it amazing how close it was to a five-year war?

Let the conspiracy theories begin—or does this evidence actually support the theory that the Franklin D. Roosevelt administration anticipated a Pearl Harbor type of event? What Congressman would have the notion to object to this *patriotic* gesture?

Nowadays, socialists don't need a war to invoke one's patriotic and civic duty to willfully participate in the progressive income tax. Writing for the Brookings Institute, Vanessa S. Williamson states: "It is every American's civic duty to pay their fair share of taxes."[3] Williamson pushes her modern progressive narrative opinion of civic pride as being part of the *collective* in paying your fair share of taxes:

> Americans almost universally agree that taxpaying is a civic duty. Asked to explain what they mean by this responsibility, my interviewees describe the taxpaying obligation as a consequence of a sense of shared interest, a belief in their fellowship with others in the community. To be a taxpayer is therefore a source of pride because it is evidence that one is an upstanding, contributing member of the community.[3]

Assuredly, most Americans believe that part of the price of living in a civilized society is the requirement to pay *some* taxes. At a minimum, common defense and other very basic fundamentals of government have to be funded. Where we have gotten off track is the limitless source of revenue created from a direct tax the Founders never would have allowed, one which has enabled Congress and the federal bureaucracy to swell beyond comprehension.

Williamson is likely partly correct in her approach that Americans will, in fact, willingly pay taxes that are necessary for government to function. But, many draw the line when funding a bloated centralized government that promotes welfare dependency, gives $4 billion in cash to Iran, funds government-sponsored abortions, and operates agencies not specifically enumerated in the U.S. Constitution like the EPA, NEA, and IRS and gives subsidies to certain groups.

There is absolutely no patriotism or civic pride for many of us who write those checks to the Department of the Treasury on the fifteenth of April. It's as if we are continuing to give dope to the addict. Williamson goes so far as to classify those of us who may not agree with this brand of civic pride as racists:

> Americans understand taxpaying as a responsibility to the community and the country. But they become angry about taxes when they see their taxes as benefitting outsiders, or when they do not believe the government is acting in the public interest. For many Americans, recent immigrants are not seen as part of "us," and so are deemed undeserving of the benefits of government. At the same time, deep doubts about the functioning of government leave many angry about their tax dollars being wasted.
>
> For a substantial percentage of the population, there is only blurry line between immigrants and "illegals," "foreigners," or even "enemies." Racism and xenophobia continue to limit Americans' social solidarity. Hostility to immigrants was accompanied by an erroneous conviction that immigrants do not pay taxes; since taxpaying is

evidence of one's standing within a community, it seems outsiders and interlopers cannot be contributors. Perhaps the most important dynamic underlying my respondents' tax attitudes is the division between "us" and "them. . . ."

So, contestation over taxes tends to recapitulate other conflicts over the boundaries of the community. Racial and ethnic divisions often undercut social solidarity, reduce approval of public investment, and increase tax opposition. Times of war, by contrast, can encourage a nation to band together and bear new costs in both blood and treasure. Attitudes about taxes are about more than individual costs and benefits; they lay are the limits of social cohesion and demarcate the lines of social strife.[3]

Typical of the progressive playbook, if one is not full of civic pride about the current tax system, you must be a racist or xenophobe.

During the height of the Tea Party movement, many progressives were aghast that conservatives were digging up American Revolution history and revealing the true roots about how anti-tax our Founders really were. Consider how the alarm bells were sounding to the progressives when the *Loyola Law Review* openly states:

> Given the rise of the tea party movement, which draws strength from the historical linkage between patriotism and tax protests in the United States, the role of patriotism as a general tax compliance factor is examined in light of the extant empirical evidence. The existing research suggests that patriotism may be a weaker tax compliance factor in the United States than it is elsewhere. In light of this possibility, the tea party movement has the potential to weaken this compliance factor even more. Further, when considered in light of the broader tax morale factors that contribute to tax compliance, the tea party movement also poses a risk of destabilizing the social contract framework that underlies

our established taxpaying ethos. In order to strengthen the impact of patriotism on tax compliance and lessen any adverse impact of the tea party movement on the country's taxpaying ethos, the government should take steps to disentangle American patriotism from its anti-tax roots. Important first steps in this regard are outlined in this Article, including the creation of a voluntary "Patriotic Remittance Tax." Making such changes will strengthen the bond between taxpayers and the government and help promote a vision of American patriotism that is positively associated with taxation rather than antithetical to it.[4]

Noted here is the admission that government should take steps to "disentangle American patriotism from its anti-tax roots." The article goes on:

America is one of the most patriotic countries in the world. Yet, while we take great pride in our country's accomplishments, Americans hate paying the taxes necessary to support their government. Our aversion to taxes has become part of our national psyche, along with the unfounded belief that we are overtaxed.[4]

The progressives know America was founded as a fierce anti-tax experiment, as evidenced by their continual propaganda that espouses the more taxes you pay, the more patriotic you are: "The government should adopt the suggested tax law changes as a means of separating American patriotism from its anti-tax roots, thereby making patriotism a more potent factor in promoting tax compliance in the United States."[4]

In this same study, it is readily admitted that despite the United States showing higher levels of patriotism than other countries, it did not correlate to an increased level of tax compliance:

Interestingly, the United States showed the smallest such correlation of all the countries. That is, while higher levels of patriotism were still positively correlated with greater probabilities of high tax compliance, the relative effect was less than that in the other countries.

That is, given the high levels of tax compliance in the United States, there is a smaller pool of noncompliant taxpayers on which patriotism could act as a compliance trigger, so the impact appears lessened. While this is a plausible explanation, the study's results still leave open the possibility that patriotism is, in fact, a weaker factor in fostering tax compliance in the United States than it is elsewhere. Such a conjecture finds support from the strong historical links in the United States between patriotism and anti-tax sentiments. Could it be that America's peculiar brand of anti-tax flavored patriotism actually decreases the intrinsic impact of patriotism as a tax compliance factor in the United States?[4]

For many Americans, it's easy to love our country while hating our government. This anti-tax legacy used to be deeply ingrained in the American psyche but has been obscured by the progressives' continual assault on our heritage, primarily through our liberal public educational system and revisionist history.

From the very founding of the United States, American patriotism has been associated with anti-tax sentiment. Indeed, the rallying cry of "no taxation without representation" forms the bedrock of many Americans' understanding of why the colonies rose up in revolt. Additionally, the pioneer values of independence and individual self-reliance have contributed to a strong undercurrent distrustful of centralized government. Since the nation itself was founded as part of a tax rebellion, it is, perhaps, understandable that American patriotism has an almost schizophrenic nature embodying both loyalty to the nation as well as distrust of its government, and a concomitant reluctance to fund the operation of potentially intrusive government activities.

Beyond the Revolutionary period, anti-tax sentiment and armed tax revolts have continued to reinforce a patriotic linkage. From the Whiskey Rebellion and Shay's Rebellion (which gave impetus to reforming the Articles of

Confederation) to reenactments of the Boston Tea Party protesting modern day tax burdens, challenging the appropriateness of taxes has been seen as an act of patriotism, or conversely, as the patriotic defense of citizen rights against the tyranny of taxation. As a result of this rich history, "in the United States, anti-tax sentiments, along with anti-government sentiments generally, are an intrinsic aspect of American patriotism and national character.... Americans celebrate their patriotism and commitment to liberty through resistance—often violent resistance—to taxes." Indeed, a well-known tax protestor manifesto proudly notes that "it was tax protesters, not any political party, or judge or prosecutor who gave us our great Constitutional Republican form of government. The tax protest is more American than baseball, hot dogs, apple pie or Chevrolet!"

This popular linkage of patriotism with anti-tax sentiment has also given rise, in the modern era, to an accepted belief that patriotism has no proper role in determining a citizen's taxpaying obligations. While in the early 1900s a prevailing strain of thought branded tax evaders as unpatriotic, faithless, and detestable cowards, beginning in the 1920s, views on taxation began to shift. This body of thought began to draw a legalistic (and hence morally indifferent) distinction between tax avoidance and tax evasion. As long as a tax minimization scheme arguably was not prohibited by the letter of the law, then it was permissible, since there was no moral or patriotic duty to fund the state. Only explicitly illegal means of tax avoidance were prohibited. This amoral conception of the nature of taxation was ultimately adopted by the courts, which, even when they ruled against various taxpayer avoidance schemes, made sure to emphasize that citizens' tax obligations were legal, not patriotic, duties. Thus, the duty to pay taxes evolved into a purely legal question divorced of all moral or patriotic flavor.[4]

The effect patriotism has on the American ethos regarding historical anti-tax sentiment is exactly the opposite of the effect that government propaganda has promoted during periods of war. The Tea Party movement is the perfect and most recent example:

> The tea party movement has the potential to undermine the taxpaying ethos in the United States. Further, the relevant empirical work on patriotism as a tax morale factor hints that the anti-tax tinge of American patriotism may itself represent a weak link in maintaining a stable taxpaying ethos in the United States. Given the significant impact that the tea party movement has had on the national debate in recent years, the threat should not be ignored. Indeed, even if the tea party movement were to suddenly falter in the near future, it may have already served to further degrade patriotism as a tax morale factor in the United States and thereby increase the vulnerability of the taxpaying ethos in the United States to future challenges.[4]

The progressives were so worried about the Tea Party impact that re-ignited America's anti-tax roots, they bluntly suggest the government should consider taking "steps," including altering American's anti-tax history in schools to stop further future revolts. In other words, teaching revisionist history with the goal of accepting the socialistic progressive income tax.

> So, regardless of what the future holds for the tea party movement, the government should consider steps that will lessen or eliminate the linkage between patriotism and anti-tax sentiment in this country. While the most overt means to accomplish this in the long run would be the alteration of school textbooks to downplay the anti-tax roots of the American Revolution, few in this country would stand for such intentional slanting of how American history is presented. At the other extreme, patriotic appeals for increased taxes could be mounted by the government. However, while such appeals have had some success in times of war, their efficacy is likely to be short lived and

limited to wartime situations. Indeed, politicians who have been brave enough to advocate for tax increases by trying to explain the genuine need for increased funds have routinely suffered adverse consequences at the ballot box. So, rational appeals to the need to raise taxes to combat a looming debt crisis are likely to be either eschewed by politicians fearful of losing their jobs or rejected by voters based on their ingrained anti-tax mindset.

If American patriotism is to be effectively separated from its anti-tax undercurrent, the approach must nurture the growth of a new conception of American patriotism from within the ranks of those currently associating patriotism with anti-tax fervor. This section presents two possible approaches that could help plant the seeds from which a pro-tax form of patriotism could grow out of the present anti-tax framework. Both ideas draw on the tea party movement's commitment to smaller government and fiscal responsibility, and they both try to link those goals with positive incentives to pay taxes. That is, if the desire for a small, fiscally responsible government is the primary motivator of the tea party movement, then it may be possible to co-opt that motivating force into one promoting tax compliance, and thereby shift the patriotic feelings of those involved in the movement away from the anti-tax undercurrent.[4]

The federal government established a "voluntary public debt payment plan" wherein self-described *patriotic* citizens could contribute a sum of their choosing that would be tax deductible on their current year taxes. This program was meant to provide the means for Americans to patriotically contribute more to fund the government and retire their enormous debt.

Based on government data, this program has been a dismal failure. For all the ranting by progressives to "pay your fair share," it would seem most do not have any desire to be "more patriotic" when it comes to taxes.

The U.S. Treasury Department reports that in 2018, only $775,654.63 was voluntarily paid to the U.S. Treasury to retire the public debt.[5]

To put that in context, America's total debt as of December 2018 was almost $22 trillion dollars. The amount voluntarily and *patriotically* paid to retire that debt in 2018 amounted to approximately .000000035 percent of the debt owed.

For further context, here is a sample list of notable progressives. They obviously have the means to be more *patriotic* than others, as they could have individually paid more than the $775,000 total that was paid in, which would have gone to retire the debt! Note: these are published salaries for the latest year publicly available, and do not include net-worth calculations:

- George Clooney (Actor) $285 Million[6]
- Sundar Pichai (Google) $150 Million[7]
- Katy Perry (Singer) $83 Million[6]
- Leslie Moonves (CBS) $69 Million[7]
- Hillary Clinton (Politician) $28 Million[8]
- Barack Obama (Politician) $20 Million[9]
- Satya Nadella (Microsoft) $18 Million[7]
- Nicolas Cage (Actor) $16 Million[10]
- Nancy Pelosi (Politician) $2 Million[11]
- Kamala Harris (Politician) $1.7 Million[12]
- Bernie Sanders (Politician) $1 Million[13]
- Elizabeth Warren(Politician) $913 Thousand[14]

In researching who voluntarily paid into the government's debt payment option, no data is available on individual donors. (Those would only be disclosed on someone's individual tax returns.) Statistically speaking, it is logical, however, to assume that some names on this very small sampling of progressives—who are publicly in favor of soaking the rich—would rather have you be more patriotic than they are.

Americans should embrace our anti-tax history and not let the progressives rewrite history and textbooks to cultivate a subservient, socialistic society.

9

---★---

THE BENEVOLENT STATE VIA THE INCOME TAX

"The champions of socialism call themselves progressives, but they recommend a system which is characterized by rigid observance of routine and by a resistance to every kind of improvement. They call themselves liberals, but they are intent upon abolishing liberty. They call themselves democrats, but they yearn for dictatorship. They call themselves revolutionaries, but they want to make the government omnipotent. They promise the blessings of the Garden of Eden, but they plan to transform the world into a gigantic post office."

—Ludwig Von Mises (1881–1973)
Austrian Economist

T he social justice intent of the progressives to design a progressive income tax system that redistributes wealth on its own and outside of typical welfare means-testing is alive and well.

One area of rampant abuse appears to be the use of the earned income tax credits (EITC) and the additional child tax credits (ACTC).

Our federal government is taking billions of dollars and paying it out to those who don't deserve it. Politico, a left-leaning alternative news site, states:

> The IRS paid out at least $5.9 billion in improper payments
> of the additional child tax credit in the fiscal year 2013, or

91

about 25 percent to 30 percent of total payments, the Treasury inspector general for tax administration said Tuesday.

What many call a nonsensical law creates the situation.

The IRS requires workers to file tax returns regardless of their immigration status. Authorized immigrants use their Social Security numbers to do so. But those ineligible to receive them can instead get a nine-digit individual taxpayer identification number to use for tax reporting purposes. Experts say undocumented workers comprise the great majority of people using such numbers. About 3 million tax forms filed in 2010 had these ITINs.[1]

And here's the most egregious fact of this entire debacle. Both parties know about it, but the progressives in both parties allow it to happen, many championing the cause. "The IRS has said the law doesn't give it the legal authority to deny the credit to unauthorized workers."[1]

Most of these payments have been made to illegal aliens who have claimed dependents in other countries, primarily Mexico, who have never likely stepped foot in the United States. Is it any wonder why there are thousands of people lined up in caravans to overwhelm our broken asylum system? Many of these tax credits, paid in the form of "refunds," are more than many of the individuals in the caravans will make in a year—or possibly a lifetime in their home countries.

The migrant caravans are nothing more than a modern-day Gold Rush!

The qualifications an illegal alien has to make to qualify for an EITC or ACTC are minimal, and it would appear Congress and the IRS have really no incentive to amend the requirements:

Qualifying child (QC) errors occur when the adult claimant has no right to claim a child as a dependent. Some 30 percent of erroneous EITC tax returns have QC errors, and returns with these errors account for around half of all erroneous overclaim dollars. There are three main types of qualifying child errors: errors concerning the age of the child, errors concerning the relationship of the adult to the child, and false residency claims by the adult claimant.

The most important of these categories is false residency claims. An adult EITC claimant is not required to financially support the child he claims. However, in order to claim EITC benefits for a child, the adult claimant must reside with the child for at least half of the year. A false residence claim occurs when the tax filer did not actually reside with the child either for the specified period or at all.[2]

Much of the IRS-produced data for these studies is dated and runs significantly behind the migration curve that has been seen in recent years. Finding relevant data after 2015 from the IRS on this subject is difficult, if not impossible. Abuse from filers who claim dependents who would not meet requirements for either credit is rampant, and likely growing:

> Multi-family households with children that contain at least two adult biological relatives filing separate tax returns are about 11 percent of the 48 million households with children. (A spouse or cohabiting partner is not considered a relative for purposes of this calculation.) Approximately one-tenth of these households engage in "sorting," or gaming behavior in which one or more children are assigned to a relative other than the parent or closest relative in order to obtain tax benefits. This means that roughly 530,000 households with children are engaged in benefit gaming within the households. (This implies that the number of relatives receiving EITC benefits as a result of false residence claims is likely to greatly exceed the number of relative filers who actually reside with mother and child.)[2]

An investigative report from a tax preparer/whistleblower in Indiana on WTHR, Channel 13 provided explosive testimony on the abuse of these credits by illegal aliens. This is part of the transcript from Bob Segall's "Tax Loophole" investigation:

13 Investigates discovered that millions of illegal immigrants are getting bigger tax refunds than you are and it's all because of a massive tax loophole that costs billions and you're paying for it. Our investigative reporter Bob Segall has spent the past three months uncovering this problem right here in Indiana. He tells us tonight how the IRS is simply handing out your tax dollars to people who don't even live here.

We are not showing his face and he does not want you to know his name but this longtime tax consultant does want you to know what he's discovered.

"There's not a doubt in my mind there's huge fraud taking place here," says the whistleblower who does not allow his face to be recorded.

He came to 13 Investigates to blow the whistle on a nationwide problem with a huge price tag. We're talking about a multi-billion-dollar fraud scheme here that is taking place. The scheme involves illegal immigrants' illegal immigrants who are filing tax returns. You see everyone who earns money in the U.S. is required to pay taxes. The IRS says it's even required for those who are working here illegally. Of course, undocumented workers aren't supposed to have a social security number so for them to pay taxes the IRS created what's called an ITIN. It's an individual taxpayer identification number while that may have seemed like a good idea it's now backfiring in a big way.

"I think the public needs to know about this," this tax preparer says.

His office has been flooded by illegal workers who have figured out a loophole it allows them to use their ITIN numbers to get huge refunds from the IRS the loophole. It is called the additional child tax credit. It's meant to help working families who have children living at home, but 13 Investigates has found many undocumented workers claiming the tax credit for kids who live in Mexico. And we're talking lots of kids. We've seen 10, 12 and it's most times nieces and nephews on these tax returns. The more you put on there the more you get back. Our whistleblower says he has thousands of examples. He showed us some of them after crossing out all identifying information.

"Here's a tax return where you show an $11,000 refund. On this return, we're claiming seven nieces and nephews. Here's a return right here where we've got a ten thousand three-hundred-dollar refund for nine nieces and nephews," says Segall.

"I can bring out stacks and stacks, it's just so easy it's ridiculous," says the whistleblower.

This undocumented worker says it is easy mucho dinero. He agreed to talk with me and a translator as long as we didn't reveal his identity he admitted his address is being used to file tax returns by for other undocumented workers who don't even live here and what's more those four workers claim 20 children live inside this one trailer home in southern Indiana and as a result the IRS sent the illegal immigrants tax refunds totaling $29,680.00.

But we saw only one of the little girls who lives here — what about the 20 kids claimed as tax deductions? "No, they don't live here," said the undocumented worker.

And have those children ever lived here?" asked the accompanying reporter. "No, never," the illegal alien answered.

"Some people who say that they shouldn't be getting that money for children who don't live in the United States?" asked Segall through an interpreter.

"The opportunity is there and they can give it to him why not take advantage of it?" stated the illegal alien.

Other undocumented workers in Indiana told me the same thing. Their families are also collecting tax refunds for children who do not live in this country.

"Have the children in Mexico ever lived here with you?" Segall asked a second illegal alien who agreed to be interviewed.

"All of those children are in Mexico, yeah," stated the second illegal alien through the interpreter.

95

While this may come as a surprise to you, the tax preparer says it should be no surprise to the government. The IRS has to know what is going on here. The IRS does know what's going on. 13 investigates has proof the agency has known about this problem for years and officials here in IRS headquarters have done absolutely nothing to stop it.

The magnitude of the problem has grown exponentially. Russell George is the US Treasury Department's Inspector General for tax administration. His agency has repeatedly warned the IRS the additional child tax credits (ACTC) are being abused by undocumented workers. The inspector general audit reports show over the past decade the abuse has skyrocketed and is now costing American taxpayers more than $4 billion dollars. Keep in mind we're talking about $4 billion per year.

It's very troubling he says even more troubling the IRS has not taken action despite report after report from the inspector general. We have made recommendations to them as to how they could address this and they have not taken sufficient action. What does the IRS have to say about all this? Well I called and emailed for weeks and I even went straight to IRS headquarters in Washington to get answers, but the agency said none of its 100,000 employees had time to meet with me for an interview.

Apparently, the IRS doesn't have time to respond to some tax preparers either. Last year our whistleblower noticed dozens of undocumented workers had used phony documents and false income to claim tax credits. He reported all of it to the IRS.

"These were fraudulent 100% false tax returns and you told the IRS that?" Segall asked the whistleblower.

"Yes."

"Any response from the IRS?" asked Segall.

"Absolutely none. We never heard a thing. The IRS knows about this and they're letting it happen," stated the whistleblower.

"Is it okay to leave the system as is?" asked Segall of the IRS Inspector General.

"No, it is not. $4 billion dollars a year. Once the money goes off the door it's near impossible for the IRS to get it back," stated Russell.

There's one more number I want you to think about. Two million. That is the number of undocumented workers right now who are getting tax refunds because of this loophole the IRS claims it can't do a thing about it, unless it gets permission from Congress.[3]

The IRS Inspector for Tax Administration stated on July 7, 2011: "Individuals who are not authorized to work in the United States were paid $4.2 billion in refundable credits."[4]

As recently as 2016, the Center for Immigration studies writes:

But the big attraction for filing early is not the new Obamacare tax break, which simply reduces the amount owed, it is the Old Faithful of tax breaks that illegal aliens can access: The Additional Child Tax Credit (ACTC). Illegals filing their income taxes can claim the ACTC if they have (or claim to have) children in the United States. This tax credit, unlike virtually all others, can result in a negative income tax payment. That means that no taxes will be collected from the individual, but he or she will get a check in the mail for all taxes withheld plus a bonus for the credit, as my colleague Jim Edwards has reported in the past.

The ACTC is well worth filing for; it can be as high as $1,000 per child claimed and proving the existence of a child is all too easy, with an ID number issued all too casually by the IRS, as we reported a couple of years ago. This is now called the TIN (tax identification number) and, in the immediate past at least, it was issued in such a sloppy way that the process was roundly criticized by the inspector general of taxation for the Department of the Treasury.

There are at least three kinds of children that an illegal can claim for the ACTC: actual citizen kids living in this country; actual children living abroad, but claimed to be living in the United States; and, at the bottom of the ladder, nonexistent children. The IRS has created a system that makes it very hard to distinguish between these three classes.[5]

When determining qualifications for certain welfare benefits, Congress has never designed a method for means-testing in order to take the generous EITC or ACTC credit refunds into consideration. In other words, despite these billions of dollars paid to those who legitimately qualify under the law—or those who don't—these payments do not impact a recipients' determination for qualification of other federal welfare payments such as SNAP, WIC, and subsidized housing, or other state or federal welfare programs too numerous to mention.

10

★

COMPLIANCE COSTS—PAYING FOR YOUR

LOSS OF FREEDOMS

"The goal of socialism is communism."

—Vladimir Lenin (1870–1924)
Russian President
Father of Communism

How much time do you spend preparing to file your income taxes? If you are taking itemized deductions, this is not just an early April ritual. It involves keeping receipts, mileage, and other unproductive and mundane tasks so that you or your tax preparer can file your best efforts at an accurate tax return.

If we were to add up the total time it takes for individuals, businesses, or corporate taxpayers to comply with an increasingly complex tax code, the costs are massive.

Unbelievably, the total cost of the progressive income tax compliance in America exceeds $409 billion and exceeds the GDP (Gross Domestic Product) of 162 nations.[1,2]

The complexity of the income tax has grown to mythical proportions. As mentioned earlier, as of 2016, the Internal Revenue Code stood at 3.8 million words, representing 77,000 pages. But this complexity is only part of the problem. In addition to these whopping but depressing statistics, there are also 7.7 million words in tax regulations and approximately 60,000 pages of tax-related case law.[2] The *Tax Foundation* states:

According to the latest estimates from the Office of Information and Regulatory Affairs, Americans will spend more than 8.9 billion hours complying with IRS tax filing requirements in 2016. This is equal to nearly 4.3 million full-time workers doing nothing but tax return paperwork. The majority of the 8.9 billion hours will be spent complying with U.S. business (2.8 billion hours) and individual income (2.6 billion hours) tax returns.[2]

In lost productivity alone and put in terms of dollars, the 8.9 billion hours also exceed the gross product of thirty-six states. The hidden cost of tax compliance is even greater than the $409 billion estimated. The Mercatus Center of George Mason University reports that another $28 billion was spent in lobbying efforts for special loopholes and tax giveaways.[3]

To put the waste of the tax burden into further context, these are estimates from the National Taxpayers Union:

> The money lost to tax compliance is greater than the combined revenues of Apple and Google parent-company Alphabet, more than the revenues of J.P. Morgan Chase, Wells Fargo, and Bank of America combined. It outstrips the total GDP of all but 35 other countries, including Finland, Portugal, and Greece. In other words, we flush down the drain of tax compliance not just entire companies-worth of productivity, but entire countries-worth.

> We know this time and out-of-pocket burden because the Paperwork Reduction Act of 1990 requires each federal agency that collects information from the public to track how much time it takes to respond and also the amount of any related personal expenses. It may not be surprising to learn that the tax system is responsible for a major portion of the government's paperwork burden, but the degree to which the tax agency impacts the country is astonishing: the time spent complying with the IRS's paperwork budget represents 71 percent of the federal government's total 11.4 billion-hour imposed time burden. The IRS generates 99

percent of the Treasury's entire burden. Among federal
cabinet departments, the Department of Health and Human
Services comes in a far distant second place, imposing 1.4
billion in compliance hours.[4]

The basic complexity required of an American citizen just to file
their taxes has grown exponentially to unthinkable proportions.
Americans now use paid tax preparers more than at any time in
history.

> With this bewildering array of forms, instructions,
> regulations, and guidance, it is no wonder that so many
> people seek help filing their taxes. But the IRS limits the
> guidance it provides to taxpayers who call the agency with
> tax questions: entire areas of tax law are "out of scope" for
> telephone tax law assistance. The IRS lists dozens of tax
> forms and topics for which it will not provide live assistance,
> including but not limited to international issues, the
> alternative minimum tax, trusts, and capital gains. Many of
> these include what people might generally assume to be
> simple questions. One likely reason for this is that studies in
> years past found that many taxpayers received wrong
> information when they called the IRS for assistance.
>
> This explains the IRS survey of taxpayers which found
> that tax preparers are more highly valued as a source of tax
> advice and information than IRS representatives. And
> demand for tax assistance has increased: The IRS estimates
> that 56 percent of forms were submitted with the help of a
> paid preparer and another 34 percent of filers used tax
> preparation software. The tax preparation industry has seen
> steady growth as a result. According to the market research
> firm IBISWorld, the tax preparation industry generated
> over $11 billion in revenue in 2017, and was comprised of
> 319,139 employees (up from 313,311 employees in 2016)
> across 135,331 businesses (compared to 131,629 in 2016).
> And the overall cost continues to climb . . . . For several
> years, National Taxpayers Union and National Taxpayers
> Union Foundation have tracked the average fee charged by

H&R Block, one of the largest such preparation businesses in the country, preparing one in every seven U.S. tax returns. Perhaps not surprisingly, those fees have steadily increased along with the system's complexity.[3]

It should be noted that even after adjusting the $27.36 average fee from 1980 for inflation (equal to $87.56 in 2018 dollars), the cost of return preparation has nearly tripled since then (now averaging $237.81), suggesting that the growth in tax complexity is outpacing even the technological and administrative improvements that have been made to professional preparation firms in that time.[4]

Now, imagine the IRS, in their compassion, has decided to adopt a "return-free" system in which they fill out your tax form and issue it to you for signature and payment. Not possible? It is strongly being considered:

> Equally concerning is another long-standing scheme called the "Return-Free" system, which would have the IRS send pre-filled tax forms to citizens for their signatures. Advocates of this proposal point to countries such as Great Britain, Sweden, and Spain where this has been implemented, but fail to note that their tax systems are far simpler than in the U.S., or that it could require significant additional reporting mandates on employers that "would fall disproportionately on small businesses" In addition, the system could potentially short-change taxpayers of considerable savings if they were to complete returns themselves or with private assistance. Worse, many Americans would likely be intimidated into submitting to the IRS's supposed "voluntary" procedure out of fear that not doing so would provoke government retaliation. And, those taxpayers who dare challenge the information that the government pre-filled for them will have to run the gauntlet of the IRS's ineffective customer service.
>
> Furthermore, as we've seen with the concern over private data from online social media services, if the IRS provides forms to complete online, all actions of the

taxpayer—including keystrokes made while filing—could be monitored by the tax agency. Perfectly innocent mistakes a filer corrected while completing the forms could be interpreted by the IRS as grounds for follow-up examinations.[4]

The IRS, despite the substantial growth in the complexity of the income tax code, is still mired in outdated technology. It is easy to get lost in the bureaucratic entanglement of the IRS's massive workforce—or worse, get harassed by them for *their* mistakes.

Despite the phone service improvements, significant problems remain for those callers who get through to an IRS representative. GAO reports that the two oldest, legacy database systems in the entire federal government are maintained by the IRS. The Individual Master File and the corresponding Business Master File track the data of hundreds of millions of tax accounts and were coded on an outdated, low-level assembly language from the 1950s, all of which was stored on magnetic tapes. Major, multi-billion-dollar attempts to modernize the system in 1988 and 1997 failed. In recent years, funding for major system upgrades had to compete with the rollout of massive new tax enforcement regimes through the Affordable Care Act and the Foreign Account Tax Compliance Act. Plans are still being considered to replace the Master File systems, but a timetable is uncertain.

Incidentally, any taxpayers facing an issue with the IRS would be well-advised to submit a Freedom of Information Act Request for a copy of their IMF, and to consult a tax expert to help decipher the alpha-numeric codes that are used to enter transaction, form, and location data into the system. The Master File systems also have size limitations, necessitating the creation of the Automated Non-Master File (ANMF) system in 1991 to account for transactions in amounts over the limit (prior to 1991 these were still tracked on paper ledgers). Despite ANMF's name, the accounts are processed manually. This extra layer of recordkeeping can lead to inconsistencies that impact taxpayer rights: The Treasury Inspector General for Tax Administration identified discrepancies between taxpayer address or taxpayer representative information between the Master File and the ANMF.

In last year's tax complexity study, we wrote that, in total, the IRS operates at least 60 different case management systems. National Taxpayer Advocate Nina Olson clarified that there are "between 60 and approximately 200 different case management systems" and they lack integration. This means that when a concerned taxpayer gets through to an IRS representative, that agent might not have access to that person's file. This adds to the taxpayer's wait time and aggravation as the representative tries to figure out who in the bureaucracy would be able to access the needed information. The IRS is working on a new "Enterprise Case Management System," but it will be several years before it is brought online . . . or whether taxpayers find out if it ended up like previous attempts to roll out technological upgrades that were ultimately unworkable despite billions of dollars invested in the programs.[4]

I have firsthand experience with requesting Freedom of Information requests (FOIA) from their IMF Individual Master Files and other data that the IRS tracks. They simply ignore my requests, and there is no recourse for the American citizen.

And, it's no better for corporations that typically have staff, tax law firms, and CPA firms to manage the menagerie of tax code idiosyncrasies. According to the *Weekly Standard*: "General Electric, one of the largest corporations in America, filed a whopping 57,000-page federal tax return earlier this year but didn't pay taxes on $14 billion in profits. The return, which was filed electronically, would have been 19 feet high if printed out and stacked."[5]

The obvious question is: Why does the progressive income tax code have to be so complex? These "loss of productivity" numbers are not lost on Congress. They all know them. How could something so obvious for so long never get permanently fixed?

The answer is: They don't want to fix it.

Why?

If you remember back in Chapter 9, it was discussed that the progressive income tax is primarily meant for social justice, welfare, and income redistribution. But, the progressive income tax code is so complex that the public is engrossed by fear of complying; therefore, its true purpose is hiding in plain sight.

Politicians and lobbyists have the now-constitutional authority to reward and punish individuals or industries—with new regulations added regularly. And, instead of an organized effort to destroy the progressive tax code, an entire industry (with significant lobbying teams) has grown to facilitate and help expand the complexity.

What keeps Americans from demanding Congress pull it out by its roots? Progressive and socialistic ideology from both parties.

The perception of soaking the rich is good for votes for both parties trying to win the lower and middle classes and ethnic voting populations. The progressive income tax has a self-perpetuating body of politicians that take money from lobbyists to keep the status quo.

According to Open Secrets, leading tax preparer H&R Block spent over $4 million in lobbying efforts in 2018. H&R Block, its executives, and affiliates also spent over $358,000 in political contributions—with the largest donations going to Democrats Claire McCaskill, Emanuel Cleaver, Blaine Luetkemeyer, Sherrod Brown, Kamala Harris, Elizabeth Warren, and Maxine Waters. But, H&R Block makes sure the other side of the aisle is also greased, contributing to Republicans Kevin McCarthy, Kevin Brady, and Dean Heller. Overall, H&R Block is responsible for 196 direct campaign contributions to candidates, some were not even up for election in 2018.[6]

Since 1990, H&R Block has given Democrats $1.57 million and Republicans $1.34 million. They have also contributed over $1.87 million to various PACs (political action committees).[6] H&R Block also gives generously and directly to the Democrats Reshaping

American PAC, as well as to the Democratic Congressional Campaign Committee.

Even more alarming is H&R Block's contribution of $70,000 directly to the committee that writes tax laws, the House Ways and Means Committee, chaired by Republican Kevin Brady, in 2018.

When examining the actuals bills that H&R Block lobbied for in 2018, seven out of eight were directly related to American citizens' interaction with the tax code and the IRS:

- *S.912*   *Tax Filing Simplification Act*
- *H.R.3860*   *IRS Data Verification Modernization Act*
- *H.R.5444*   *Taxpayer First Act*
- *H.R.5445*   *21st Century IRS Act*
- *S.3278*   *Protecting Taxpayers Act*
- *S.3246*   *Taxpayer First Act of 2018*

Does H&R Block benefit from simplifying the tax code—or, is business booming because the complexity grows annually? Twenty-one of H&R Block's twenty-five top lobbyists were former federal government employees. The company's sales revenue now tops $3.16 billion per year.[6]

Consider the top auditing and consulting firms in the world that most Fortune 500® companies use to file audited financials and corporate tax returns. The complicated progressive income tax would seem to help these major firms.

Firm	2018 Revenues (billions)	2018 Lobbying Totals (millions)	2018 Political Contributions (millions)	2018 Lobbyists from Gov't
Deloitte	$ 43.20	$ 4.64	$ 2.38	25 of 29
PWC	$ 41.30	$ 2.91	$ 3.20	23 OF 32
EY	$ 34.80	$ 3.57	$ 3.66	18 OF 25
KPMG	$ 29.00	$ 1.41	$ 2.25	7 of 11
Totals	$ 148.30	$ 12.53	$ 11.49	73 of 97 (75%)

Source: OpenSecrets.Org

These firms spent millions in lobbying and political contributions, and 75 percent of their lobbyists are *former* federal government employees. When all the pieces are put together and we see the type of influence the tax industry has on our elected officials, it's not much of an intellectual leap to see why the progressive tax code continues to get more complex every year.

Besides the redistribution aspect of the progressive income tax, Congress also gets to choose winners and losers via the tax code, and, thanks to lobbyists, billions of dollars continue to influence its complexity.

Take the home mortgage interest deduction for example. This deduction typically gets the most heated response from a multitude of special interests when flattening the progressive income tax or in attempting to simplify it. The home construction industry, realtors, and banks are heavily invested in the home mortgage interest deduction, and any mention of closing that deduction garners intense lobbying and outcries.

It's almost *un-American*....

What's un-American is having a progressive income tax that is so complex, convoluted, and overly burdensome, it has created its own industry that's larger than the GDP of many countries.

11

---★---

THE PROGRESSIVE'S SECRET WEAPON: FEAR

"An IRS audit is like an autopsy without the benefit of dying first."

—Unknown

Every year, Americans are required to affix their signature to a document, attesting under penalty of perjury (among many other penalties) they commit that their taxes are done to the letter of the law, under the 77,000-page tax code: "Under penalties of perjury, I declare that I have examined this return and accompanying schedules and statements and, to the best of my knowledge and belief, they are true, correct, and complete."[1]

Just the *act* of signing that document gives many Americans heart palpitations. *Did I do it right? Did I take too many deductions, even if they were legal? Do I have all the receipts in case I'm audited?*

The IRS has the power to destroy lives simply with a letter, phone call, or visit. They can take your business. They can empty your bank account. They can take your home. Even if a professional tax preparer is used, there is no escaping the IRS. Ultimately, the responsibility of an accurate return is on the taxpayer. Seldom are preparers penalized for inaccurate returns unless the preparer has a track record of professional incompetence—or worse.

In the case of a criminal CPA in the Houston area who was somehow able to talk his personal clients into sending him their payroll withholding, personal, and business income tax return payments, the IRS showed no mercy. These clients thought they had been paying in, only to find out that the IRS made them pay in *again*. Yes, the CPA went to prison, but the IRS showed no mercy went it came to the collecting, including charging the unfortunate victims of the crooked CPA interest and penalties.

There were many years where I would get an anxiety attack from the simple act of walking to our mailbox to retrieve the day's mail. The cause? That dreaded large, white envelope.

The progressive's secret weapon is *fear*.

If you've ever been notified of an IRS audit, or of the results of one, you know the envelope of which I'm speaking. The fear for me was so deep, I wouldn't get the mail. For that reason, we would have an irritated postal service employee knock on our door every week or so with her arms full of mail that would no longer fit into our mailbox.

Over the years, we became "enemies of the state" as we had to hire high-priced but competent professionals to fight on our behalf during the onslaught we encountered over the eight years of the Obama administration. Fortunately, that fear eventually dissipated as it turned into outrage. But, for millions of Americans, a notice from the IRS can strike terror into the average taxpayer. This is especially true of those being audited for the first time.

Since 2014, the IRS has conducted 4.43 million individual tax return audits. Although that puts your likelihood of an audit at about .6 percent, the chances of an audit grow significantly as your AGI (adjusted gross income) increases, especially those north of $100,000 in annual income.[2]

According to Syracuse University's TRAC program, which monitors various government agencies since 1992, the IRS has issued more than 60 million liens, assigned 17 million levies, and has had 73,000 actual seizures of property.[3]

The IRS can seize property and bank accounts and put you out of your home. Because of the special powers granted by Congress and the ability to nullify the Bill of Rights, the IRS can enforce the abusive progressive tax code virtually without oversight. Even if the IRS mistakenly or erroneously assesses a tax levy, the citizen has to pay the taxes first, then fight the IRS in tax court to recover them. There is absolutely no due process.

These unfettered elements of enforcement and the well-earned reputation of IRS enforcement agents are the roots of the *fear*.

According to the *Washington Business Journal*, 59 percent say that fear of audit influences how they report their taxes.[4]

Under the auspices of drug trafficking and money laundering, the IRS has increased its weaponization program. For those who defend this weaponization, it is typically justified with historical context to the IRS's successful criminal prosecution of Al Capone, a.k.a. Public Enemy No. 1. Since Capone continued to outsmart the FBI, the government was able to prosecute Capone via an IRS Special Investigation unit, ultimately capturing him through his accountant.

The IRS used a 1927 Supreme Court case (*United States v. Sullivan*) wherein it was ruled that illegally earned income was subject to income tax. Capone was sentenced to eleven years. What the FBI couldn't accomplish on its own was conveniently circumvented using the progressive income tax provisions.[5]

Since that era, the IRS has always had a special crimes unit and has actively pursued an increase in their overall scope of jurisdiction under the guise of prosecuting money laundering, organized crime, drug trafficking, and various other criminal activities. It's evident to see the IRS's fingerprints in overly broad and invasive banking laws, including specifically the Patriot Act and the National Defense Authorization Act.

The natural outcome of this increase in scope was the growth in the weaponization of the IRS under the Obama administration.

In 2014, the organization Open the Books published an oversight study entitled "The Militarization of America: Non-Military Federal Agencies Purchases of Guns, Ammo, and Military-Style Equipment." The report states: "The Internal Revenue Service, with its 2,316 Special Agents spent nearly $11 million on guns, ammunition, and military-style equipment."[6]

Further, the report states, the IRS's total number of dollars spent on weaponry in 2014 was double the amount spent in 1995. The number of non-defense department federal officers authorized to make arrests and carry firearms (200,000) now exceeds the number of U.S. Marines (182,000).[7]

The IRS's total workforce as of 2017 was 97,717 employees. Of these totals, there were 13,036 revenue agents and 5,152 revenue officers.[3] The IRS employs more people than Exxon, Nike, Delta Airlines, Google, Southwest Airlines, Intuit, Mastercard, Cisco, Monsanto, USAA, Northrop Grumman, Raytheon, Nationwide Insurance, Nordstrom, Aetna, Boston Scientific, Netflix, Travelers, American Express, Kimberly-Clark, Dow Chemical, ADP, McKesson, Chevron, State Farm, Archer Daniels, Pfizer, Cigna, Allstate, Facebook, Coca-Cola, Rite-Aid, Time Warner, Capital One, John Deere, Hewlett-Packard, Phillip-Morris, Halliburton, Cummins, Kohl's, Visa, Kimberly-Clark, PG&E, CenturyLink, General Mills, Goodyear, Texas Instruments, CBS, MasterCard, and Qualcomm, just to name a few.[8]

The IRS has the seventh largest number of employees in the federal government, only behind Veterans Affairs, the Departments of Defense and Agriculture, and the Army, Navy, and Air Force. They literally have an army of their own.[9]

The IRS budget for the fiscal year 2018 was $10.975 billion. The IRS would rank #279 on the Fortune 500® based on its budget. If it were to be ranked on revenue collected in 2016 ($3.3 trillion), it would be number one, and Walmart would be a very distant second at $500 billion.[10] According to the Department of the Treasury:

> The IRS remains one of the most cost-effective investments in the federal government and resources invested in the IRS increase revenue collections. This unique and critical role is vital to the functioning of the U.S. Government and to keeping the nation and economy strong. In FY 2016, the IRS collected more than $3.3 trillion in tax revenue, processed more than 244 million tax returns and other forms, and issued more than $426 billion in tax refunds.
>
> As collections continue to increase, the IRS remains one of the most efficient tax administrators in the world. For every $100 collected in taxes, the IRS spends only thirty-five cents. The IRS enforcement programs collected

more than $54.3 billion in FY 2016, a return on investment (ROI) of about $5 to $1. The ROI estimate does not include the revenue effect of the deterrence value of these investments and other IRS enforcement programs.[10]

Note the IRS's ROI calculation shown in the previous paragraph of $5 collected to $1 spent on collection; they are rather proud of their enforcement programs, bragging about the return on investment. This shows how effective they are in tax collections when the citizenry has been stripped of their Bill of Rights.

Conversely, a 35 percent collection cost on taxes from a businessman's perspective is extremely subpar when you have the entire weight of this Gestapo-style machine behind them with $10 billion-plus in resources. It proves, even with the constant fear of an audit and other unthinkable measures the IRS has at their disposal, Americans still have a hard time maneuvering around a dynamic and complex, 77,000-page tax code.

The IRS has asked for $122 million in raises in new budget requests, with the majority of those raises going to the Enforcement division. Currently, most income tax returns are filed electronically (over 90 percent according to the latest figures),[10] but this doesn't mean completing a tax return is any easier. It only means more people now have to use a professional tax preparer, who will typically file their return for them electronically.

Even Mark J. Kohler of *Entrepreneur*, a respected print and online small business magazine, played to the fears of taxpayers—who had legitimate deductions to claim. In "The Top Ten Ways to Avoid an IRS or State Audit," Kohler advised against taking them:

> When you file a tax return, you also indicate the industry that you work in. This allows the IRS to categorize your expenses and look for abnormal expense levels compared to your income. Obviously, you would never increase an expense because "it wouldn't be noticed." But you certainly should also consider reducing an expense if it is far too high and will stand out.[11]

Amazingly, they also recommended changing a business from a sole proprietor to a partnership or corporation to avoid Schedule C expenses. This is simply not feasible for many small operators. Schedule C is also one of the last available legitimate means to take all deductions a small business owner is entitled to: "Having a small business is a great tax-saving strategy, but reporting it as a sole proprietorship can dramatically increase your chances of an audit. Choose instead to file as a partnership or corporation when that's economically feasible. Make that change this year."[11]

There is no public data available that reports the estimated total amount of taxes paid by Americans simply because they are afraid to take legitimate and legal deductions. Some facts from Lexington Law imply Americans fear their own government. "To find out how confident Americans are with their understanding of the U.S. tax code, we surveyed 2,000 people about their tax literacy." Major takeaways include:

- 1 in 5 (unnecessarily) keep their tax records for over 16 years.
- 33% over the age of 65 reported fears of being audited in their lifetime.
- Men are 12% more fearful of getting audited than women.
- 25% are afraid of an IRS audit.

According to the IRS themselves, there is ample reason for Americans' fear of an audit. In the *Internal Revenue Service Data Book, 2017* (published in September 2017), the IRS stated there were 1.1 million audits that year that resulted in additional collections by the IRS of an additional $3.7 billion in taxes and penalties. A total of only $11.5 million of that amount was fought by the taxpayer.[13]

It's not hard to figure out where the fear emanates from. Every American has heard IRS audit horror stories firsthand. Rarely does a taxpayer exit an IRS audit unscathed. Even in my experience, where the IRS finds no significant taxes due, hiring CPAs or tax attorneys to fend off the audits is expensive. There is no penalty to incentivize the IRS to pay your legal and/or professional accountant's fees in audit cases where no additional taxes are due.

Despite the fact that the average IRS revenue agent's salary is $102,749 (in 2016)[14], with myriad exceeding $150,000 per year, many have no accounting backgrounds and are horribly inept.

Add IRS incompetence to tax code complexity, and you have a recipe for probably the worst tax system in the world.

A 2016 article by Megan McArdle in the *Chicago Tribune* sums it up:

> Filling out your taxes is not a matter of being good at math or accounting, or even knowing how various provisions of the tax code interact in revenue projections. It is entirely a matter of knowing what can be deducted, and how. And because our tax code is so complex, that doesn't mean "read the statute"; it means "read the statute and the case law, and develop a sense over a long experience of how agents are likely to interpret this or that during an audit."
>
> Only tax professionals can do that; the rest of us are too busy earning a living.
>
> Legal complexity does not accumulate linearly; it accumulates exponentially. When you have one law on the books and you add a second, the new law may have some unexpected interaction with the old law. With each new law, the number of potential interactions grows quickly until it passes the ability of any layman to grasp (and eventually even the professionals, which is why they're increasingly specialized). We are long past that point with the tax code.[15]

In February of 2010, software engineer and pilot Joe Stack had reached his limits of the tyranny he felt from the government and particularly the IRS. He wrote a lengthy manifesto, burned down his house, and calmly climbed into his small single-engine aircraft and flew from an Austin, Texas suburb and crashed it into an IRS building in Austin, killing himself and one IRS employee but engulfing the entire seven-story building in flames. In his manifesto, he states:

How can any rational individual explain that white elephant conundrum in the middle of our tax system and, indeed, our entire legal system? Here we have a system that is, by far, too complicated for the brightest of the master scholars to understand. Yet, it mercilessly "holds accountable" its victims, claiming that they're responsible for fully complying with laws not even the experts understand. The law "requires" a signature on the bottom of a tax filing; yet no one can say truthfully that they understand what they are signing; if that's not "duress" than what is. If this is not the measure of a totalitarian regime, nothing is.

It made me realize for the first time that I live in a country with an ideology that is based on a total and complete lie. It also made me realize, not only how naive I had been, but also the incredible stupidity of the American public; that they buy, hook, line, and sinker, the crap about their "freedom" . . . and that they continue to do so with eyes closed in the face of overwhelming evidence and all that keeps happening in front of them.[16]

While not condoning Stack's act of violence, it is not too hard to understand this draconian progressive tax system will put enough pressure on average American citizens to the point, like Stack, where they could lose all hope and resort to unthinkable acts. When people feel hopeless or like they cannot get ahead no matter what they do because their basic human rights and Liberties are being violated, these types of violent occurrences can happen and will likely continue.

The IRS has even developed a codename for those they "identify" as potential threats against the IRS; they use the acronym "PDT," which stands for "potentially dangerous taxpayer." Once a citizen receives this designation, it stays with their IRS file for a minimum of five years. In our research, we cannot find a single instance of due process allotted to an American citizen who was labeled a PDT. The only due process afforded a PDT is if he or she is indicted in criminal court.

According to a 2010 article in the *Dallas Morning News*:

Each year, the Treasury Inspector General for Tax Administration, which oversees the IRS, investigates more than 900 threats against IRS employees. Between 2001 and 2008, those threats resulted in 195 court convictions. In 2008, for example, Randy Nowak of Mulberry, Fla., was sentenced to 30 years in federal prison for trying to hire a hit man to kill the IRS employee auditing his taxes.

The IRS also has a "Potentially Dangerous Taxpayer" list that includes the names, addresses and case histories of people who have threatened, assaulted, harassed or otherwise interfered with the duties of IRS employees.

IRS spokesman Clay Sanford said he could not discuss how many people are on that list or whether Stack had been designated a potentially dangerous taxpayer.[17]

What ability does the IRS have to decide if a taxpayer is a threat? Just like with the IRS's inability to decipher their own tax code, do they even have the training to make that determination? We have all been fearful of ending up on some "list" at the IRS for repeat audits and other unpleasantries. Now, your freedom of speech could be interpreted as a "threat" by the IRS simply for voicing your opinion on an IRS assessment or interpretation of your tax return?

Not surprising, however, is the fact that even the IRS employees don't know what constitutes their own criteria for assessing a threat, according to a Treasury Inspector General report in 2013, where 79 percent of IRS employees questioned did not know the difference between a PDT (potentially dangerous taxpayer) and a "CAU" (caution upon contact) designation of a taxpayer. For instance, a CAU designation may not be any threat to an IRS employee but may be suicidal, and caution is advised when contacting. A CAU designation can also be made when a taxpayer threatens litigation or criminal or legal action against an IRS employee or the IRS itself. A full 85 percent of the IRS employees polled had not received PDT and CAU criteria and procedures training, and 71 percent of those polled by the Inspector General were not even familiar with CAU designation.[18]

What may be even more concerning is the Inspector General also measured whether the IRS properly applied PDT or CAU determination to a very small (fifteen cases) sampling of taxpayer cases. Despite over 6,649 cases that were active at the time of the report, 13.3 percent were determined to *not* meet the criteria for either PDT or CAU status. If those findings were extrapolated, 864 taxpayers (13.3 percent of the 6,649 active cases in 2013) had been improperly and unfairly labeled as a threat to IRS employees—yet, they didn't likely even know it. The Inspector General report also states, regarding IRS training guides, that:

- 90% did not include PDT criteria
- 60% had outdated material
- 70% did not include CAU criteria
- 20% indicated IRS Criminal Investigation should be contacted for an armed escort, yet this armed escort responsibility falls to the Inspector General office and not IRS Criminal Investigation[18]

We shouldn't be surprised to find this type of incompetence at any level of federal government bureaucracy; however, when it exists in a bureaucracy that can easily trample Americans' rights, it is shocking.

So, IRS agents aren't properly trained. Big surprise. Here's an example of why it matters, and of the palpable fear the IRS—as a result of the progressive income tax—strikes into people:

California CPA Melody Thornton tells Reuters that she actually talked a young woman off a ledge—all because of taxes. The woman was willing to end her life due to a mistake she'd made while completing withholdings. This situation is more common than you might suspect; the IRS has actually been sued for wrongful death due to the emotional distress caused by raids and other collection actions. IRS issues can serve as a powerful trigger for those with pre-existing mental health problems.[19]

It should also not be surprising how these two lists of taxpayers could be found on similar NDAA (National Defense Authorization Act) lists; they were denied American due process.

Imagine the "Son of Thunder" a.k.a. Patrick Henry, Samuel Adams, or Thomas Jefferson being summoned for an IRS audit wherein they had to provide the federal government access to all their personal financial records. Would they have been put on the PDT list? Would they have feared their government?

Can't imagine it? Neither can I.

Yet, the strength of the American character has evaporated under the acceptance of the progressive ideology that has been foisted by the spineless politicians from both parties. The rugged individualism, strong anti-tax sentiment, and liberty-at-all-costs mindset of our Founders have been neutered carefully by the progressives until we quiver in our own homes over the fear of an IRS audit by a socialist government.

12

★

THE HORROR STORIES

"People try to live within their income so they can afford to pay taxes to a government that can't live within its income."

— Robert Half (1918–2001)
Founder of Robert Half International

T here is no complete tale of the destruction of freedoms using the progressive income tax without some of the requisite horror stories that surround the enforcement actions foisted upon us by the socialists of both parties of this government. There are volumes of firsthand stories of criminal and incompetent behavior by the government, and particularly about the collection arm (IRS) of the Treasury Department, but, unfortunately, many aren't a matter of public knowledge.

Enforcement actions are meant to be a deterrent to those who would attempt to circumvent, cheat, or otherwise steal money from the U.S. government. Unfortunately, without protections from our Bill of Rights in tax cases, the IRS simply runs roughshod over citizens with the loud and clear message: "Don't mess with our progressive tax code and especially with the IRS."

Paul Hatz of Boston (as of this writing) is knee-deep in appealing the results of a five-year-long "nightmare audit" that recently concluded:

> *The auditor, Hatz claims, failed to send out statutory notice*
> *of deficiency letters — thus denying him "the most*

fundamental taxpayer right, the right to appeal what an auditor says," he said — and he was slapped with a personal lien for $110,000 in taxes. The liability, though, wasn't Hatz's, but rather that of the C corporation he ran — by definition, taxed separately from its proprietors.

"To add insult to injury, this 'tax' was all because the auditor miscategorized money I invested into the corp as 'income,'" Hatz said. Because of the auditor's error, not only did Hatz lose the $100,000 investment he made in his corporation, he also got a $110,000 bill from the IRS for failing to report the amount as income.

"I know this sounds crazy, and I wish I made it all up," Hatz said.

Hatz hired a tax attorney and got a congressman involved. But as a result of the financial burdens of the audit process, Hatz ended up closing his small manufacturing business, where he employed over a dozen people.

Now he collects unemployment and takes care of his child as a stay-at-home dad while he looks for work. He's dropped $60,000 in CPA and tax attorney costs and has had to declare bankruptcy. He and his spouse keep their finances separate. For all the trouble and expense Hatz has endured, the actual amount he owes is small by comparison: a measly $5,000.

The ordeal has left Hatz disillusioned with the idea of personal entrepreneurship.

"I never want to start a business again," he said. "Large corporations with teams of tax attorneys and CPAs can deal with an audit. If you get the wrong auditor and are a small business struggling to make ends meet, you are done — out of business regardless of whether you did anything wrong or not."[1]

Here are ten more IRS horror stories from "Painful Tax Return Audit Experiences":

When a Maryland dairy farmer had less than $10,000 deposited into a bank account at once, a bank teller told him it would be easier to keep his deposits low to avoid an IRS asset reporting requirement of more than $10,000. However, he was not aware that this was a crime until federal agents arrived at his farmhouse to inform him the IRS seized his money. He decided to fight back since he felt the IRS policy as it was written made him break it (and he thought the teller should have been prosecuted for misleading him). After four years of testifying before a congressional committee and appearing on worldwide television broadcasts, he became the first person to get his money back from the IRS. The IRS also updated their policy to state it would only pursue seizure of structured assets from criminal activity.

A youth soccer association is in trouble with the IRS for incorrectly filing the statuses of their referees. The association filed them as independent contractors because they pay them on a per-match basis. The IRS insists they should be filed as employees and fined them for more than $330,000.

The IRS seized a woman's equipment that she had in a beauty shop she owned. They then auctioned it off to get the money she owed them. However, it turned out she paid her taxes in full, but the IRS made an error. Though the IRS gave the equipment back to her, her business sustained significant damage.

A restaurant owner was greeted with gun-wielding IRS agents. One of his accountants for his business was fired for embezzling funds from the business. She went to the IRS and told them that her former boss was involved with gun trafficking and money laundering. It took a lot for the restaurant owner to clear his name; he even went before

Congress to complain about the damage that his reputation sustained all because of a false accusation.

A woman had to stop by the IRS office to get a problem resolved and decided to save postage by giving her Form 1040 to an IRS agent. The IRS agent looked it over and said that it was filled out wrong. The agent proceeded to correct the mistakes and then pass it along to another agent in charge of eFiling. The second agent then told her that the form was filled out wrong and the first agent must have made some mistakes. He then proceeded to correct those mistakes. The correction and re-filing process took the second agent almost 3 hours to complete. Sometime after the taxes were filed, the woman received a letter from the IRS stating that they found mistakes in her tax return and that they corrected them for her.

An owner of a gas station spent $300,000 of his money to clean up a gasoline spill that occurred at his gas station. He was lauded by the community for being a responsible person. He then claimed the cleanup cost as a business expense in his tax returns. However, the IRS disagreed because he didn't technically own the gas station when the spill occurred. However, he was ordered by the state to clean up the spill.

A woman's house burned down, and she was unable to recover her financial documents to properly file her taxes. She filed for an extension but an IRS tax notice came in several weeks later. Since she couldn't produce the necessary documents, she was fined $18,000.

A man owned a service station and a car wash. He was able to make around $70,000 a year from his business. Then he passed away, leaving his son and wife to take care of the *business. He left behind municipal bonds and a life insurance policy. However, the land that the service station stood on grew in value to around $1.7 million. They were forced to sell the service station because they were unable to pay the estate tax on the property.*

———————————

One taxpayer was audited by the IRS, which is stressful enough. The auditor, however, went beyond the ordinary and requested receipts for every single purchase made in the last 2 years, including purchases that were very small. The taxpayer couldn't produce all the receipts and had to face penalties.[2]

In "Tax Horrors That Will Give You Nightmares," Tim and Tracey Kerin went through a hellish ordeal when their company expenses triggered a tax audit. Apparently, their CPA had improperly figured their expense categories, and the couple neglected to thoroughly read the forms before signing.

"A lesson moving forward is that every business owner should spend time with their CPA and bring their Quickbooks in and go over every expense account to make sure it complies with the current tax laws," said Tim. "Also, you should visit your CPA on a regular basis and not just at tax time when the year is already closed out."

During the audit process, Tim and Tracey reached out to the Taxpayer Advocate Service (TAS) to help resolve their issue. On the IRS website, the TAS is touted as "your voice at the IRS." Their job is "to ensure that every taxpayer is treated fairly."

But when the TAS contacted the IRS on the couple's behalf, it only seemed to infuriate the IRS agent involved in their case. "She complained to our CPA and notated how upset she was on our forms," Tim recalled. "By us doing this we upset the IRS agent so she put the screws to us even harder and ignored the TAS. Our civil rights are now gone."

The Kerins then met with the Deputy Chief Counsel of the House Small Business Committee on Capitol Hill to argue their case. Tim reported that the IRS agent had completely lied about her findings because she didn't have time to review the nearly 4,000 pages of documents the couple had provided.

"The Deputy Chief Council responded that this is unfortunate," noted Tim. "Tracey said, 'Unfortunate is when my cat gets hurt! This is criminal.'"

So far, the couple has spent over 30 months trying to defend their company against an expense audit, costing them upwards of $95,000 in accounting and legal fees. "We now have to spend an additional $15,000 in appeals to defend ourselves against the lies of the IRS agent."[3]

Also in this article, freelance writer Joan Barthel had a horrific tax audit experience in 1986 while living in Manhattan with her husband. The couple had owned a summer home in Connecticut that burned down the previous year, so her husband claimed a tax deduction, triggering the audit:

"Two agents came to our apartment in New York and came in like storm troopers, just big bullies," Barthel recalled. "They said, 'Your calculations were inaccurate and you owe $14,000.'"

Barthel was shocked by how aggressively the agents behaved, treating the couple like criminals who had set out to intentionally defraud the IRS. "Starting out with those two guys—they were so gruff and mean," she said. "They came in assuming I was a criminal and had deliberately tried to cheat the United States government. It was 'guilty until proven innocent.'"

"As a layperson, you're up against this monolithic organization represented by two guys who are yelling at you," Barthel continued. "You're at a disadvantage to say the least."

The IRS demanded that Barthel provide a ridiculous amount of detail for her case. "I'm a writer, and the house was filled with books. They wanted the name and author of every book I lost in the fire. I was in tears. It was just horrible," said Barthel.

The IRS also added interest charges to the alleged debt, as if losing a house in a fire wasn't enough of a burden. The couple got a lawyer, who took their case pro bono and represented them in tax court. But the case went on for so long that the couple accumulated $2,000 in interest alone. Barthel and her husband eventually settled for about $4,000 total.

"It was horrible. I blocked it out, and I've thrown out all the paper," Barthel said.[3]

Jordan Markuson has six startups under his entrepreneurial belt, from a real estate investment company to a supplement business. (He has really built up his startup street credit.) But, while this young entrepreneur enjoyed early success, one of his startups hit a roadblock—a roadblock called the IRS. In 2003, Markuson and three other partners started a domain company, which bought and sold online domains. For years, the company ran well but, in 2011, the high revenue stream raised a red flag with Uncle Sam. *BPlans* reports his story:

"At the time, the industry was very hot for a few companies and we were doing quite well," Markuson recalls. "We often sold assets at 30 times more than what we bought them for."

"The IRS could not figure out how we were making money, so they wanted to investigate," Markuson says who received a notice in the mail that the company was going to be audited. Markuson turned to his accountant for help. Over the next six months, the IRS combed through his records. Transactions were reviewed. Accounting ledgers were checked and double-checked. Income statements were scrutinized.

"The auditing process was long and tedious," he says. "But we had excellent books. Everything was matching up. I assumed the IRS was going to close the books and move on." That wasn't the case. While Markuson says the IRS didn't find any trouble with the company's revenue, business write-offs were a problem.

"The auditor had caught me inappropriately expensing home items that were dual-use," he says. It sounds like a trivial problem, but the auditor looked at three years' worth of taxes and told Markuson he owned a substantial amount of money to the government.

"The additional tax liability and accounting costs were equal to one-third of the following year's total revenue," he says. "Paying it back becomes an uphill battle because IRS back payments are not expenses, so they are coming directly from your profit. I was putting away 70 percent of my income for taxes."

The additional tax burden destroyed his company's cash-flow and in the end, sunk the company.[4]

IRS fraud division contacted a taxpayer regarding a visit he made to the web site of a subsequently convicted abusive tax scheme promoter. Apparently, he had only visited the web site, leaving his contact information and received some promotional materials from them. He did nothing wrong, so he spoke freely with the IRS agent.

Big mistake. Not believing the taxpayer, the IRS auditor initiated a full examination of the taxpayer and all his related entities. While we've done a good job representing this taxpayer and so far the IRS has left all items unchanged, including a couple entities related to securities trading, the time and effort to respond to the IRS demands and the CPA fees might have all be avoided had the taxpayer not "volunteered" information rather than telling the IRS to speak with his CPA to get all answers.[5]

The Jewish Mother restaurant in Virginia Beach was ravaged by IRS agents armed with guns and fierce dogs. Customers were ordered to leave, and the employees were searched for drugs. Why all the fuss? The IRS believed false *statements by the restaurant's former bookkeeper (fired for embezzling money) that the Jewish Mother was the center of gun running, drug dealing and money laundering. The restaurant's owner later sued the IRS for $20 million.*[6]

Even Former U.S. Secretary of Defense Donald Rumsfeld gets confused about his taxes! After he filed his 2013 tax return, Rumsfeld still did not understand what he owed. If he gets audited, he would not know how much he should pay to the IRS. Below is a letter he wrote to the IRS on Tax Day 2014:

DONALD RUMSFELD

April 15, 2014

Internal Revenue Service
10th Street and Pennsylvania Avenue, N.W.
Washington, D.C. 20004

Dear Sir or Madame,

    I have sent in our federal income tax and our gift tax returns for 2013. As in prior years, it is important for you to know that I have absolutely no idea whether our tax returns and our tax payments are accurate. I say that despite the fact that I am a college graduate and I try hard to make sure our tax returns are accurate.

    The tax code is so complex and the forms are so complicated, that I know that I cannot have any confidence that I know what is being requested and therefore I cannot and do not know, and I suspect a great many Americans cannot know, whether or not their tax returns are accurate. As in past years, I have spent more money than I wanted to spend to hire an accounting firm to prepare our tax returns and I believe they are well qualified.

    This note is to alert you folks that I know that I do not know whether or not my tax returns are accurate, which is a sad commentary on governance in our nation's capital.

    If you have questions, let me know and I will ask our accountants to be in touch with you to try to provide any additional information you may think you need.

    I do hope that at some point in my lifetime, and I am now in my 80s, so there are not many years left, the U.S. government will simplify the U.S. tax code so that those citizens who sincerely want to pay what they should, are able to do it right, and know that they have done it right.

    I should add that my wife of 59 years, also a college graduate, has signed our joint return, but she also knows that she does not have any idea whether or not our tax payments are accurate.

Sincerely,

Donald Rumsfeld

Consider how Congress and the Justice Department, using the progressive income tax's enforcement division, has expanded on their outright invasion of basic civil liberties when it comes to asset seizures.

In May 2013, David Vocatura watched $68,000 disappear.

He was at his family's bakery in Norwich, Connecticut, when a squad of armed IRS agents filed into the store. The agents wanted to know if Vocatura and his brother Larry were trafficking drugs or running a prostitution ring. The brothers had no idea what they were talking about.

Vocatura's Bakery has been doing business for nearly a century. The brothers operate a restaurant that serves up pizza and sandwiches—which, until a few years back, only accepted cash—as well as a commercial bakery that delivers fresh Italian bread throughout the region.

Their grandfather, Frank, founded Vocatura's in Rhode Island in 1919, before the family moved it to Norwich in the 1950s.

But the IRS refused to believe Vocatura's Bakery was operating on the up and up. Agents said the business raised red flags because of a series of cash deposits in sums under $10,000, the amount at which banks are required to report transactions to the federal government. They said this behavior was consistent with a crime known as structuring, which the IRS defines as making calculated financial transactions in order to skirt reporting requirements. The agents had no evidence of other wrongdoing, but thanks to a controversial law enforcement tool known as civil asset forfeiture, they didn't need any to seize every penny in the Vocatura's bank account: $68,382.22.

Under the practice of civil forfeiture, authorities can move to permanently take property they suspect of being linked to criminal activity, without obtaining a conviction—and, in cases like the Vocatura's, without even charging the owner with a crime.

For the past three years, the brothers have been fighting to get their money back, maintaining they'd done nothing wrong. The IRS has responded by subjecting David, 53, and his brother, Larry, 69, to a series of increasingly aggressive legal maneuvers—including threats of significant prison time and additional fines—in an attempt to strong-arm them into permanently forfeiting their assets.

On Tuesday, the Institute for Justice, a libertarian public interest law firm, filed a lawsuit in U.S. District Court for the District of Connecticut on behalf of Vocatura's Bakery, demanding that the IRS promptly return their money. The suit argued that the Vocaturas were just the latest example of the government hastily seizing property, and then going to extreme and even unconstitutional lengths to justify it after the fact.

Hours after the suit was filed, the IRS said it would finally give the Vocaturas their money back. But the prosecutor didn't drop the case. Instead, he now plans to mount an expansive investigation into the bakery's finances, looking for a reason to bring criminal charges against the brothers.

It was just the latest twist in a protracted legal battle that has called into question some of the government's favorite— and most problematic—methods of taking people's money.

Structuring laws were initially designed to keep drug kingpins, terrorists, and money launderers from evading detection, but the IRS expanded their enforcement efforts in the past decade, and ensnared small business owners along the way.

At issue in the Vocaturas' case are hundreds of deposits between March 2007 and April 2013 that ranged from $7,000 to $9,900—a total of around $2.8 million. The Vocaturas say the deposited money was from the bakery's sales, as they were doing mainly cash business at the time, and they have a less suspicious explanation for why the deposits were so close to the reporting limit. David Vocatura says a representative from their local bank told

131

him that an employee had to fill out forms each time they brought in more than $10,000, so he decided to make life easier for the bank attendants by making smaller, more frequent deposits.

"I didn't know what structuring was that day, until the agent explained to me what it was," he told the Huffington Post. "We're good, hardworking people and we run a clean, legitimate business."

If the IRS has proof that the Vocaturas were deliberately structuring payments or hiding illicit proceeds, it hasn't provided it.

"We gave them all kinds of records, we've cooperated with them since Day One, personal and business information, anything they've wanted," said David Vocatura. "They checked us out."

Earlier this month, Peter S. Jongbloed, Assistant U.S. Attorney for the District of Connecticut, served the Vocaturas a grand jury subpoena calling for them to turn over every financial record from the six years between March 2007 and April 2013, so the agency could finally begin investigating the business's tax and regulatory compliance. At the time, it was the latest reminder that the government was intent on taking the brothers' assets, even if it had to change its approach three years after the fact.

On Tuesday, Jongbloed said he was proceeding with the probe ahead of possible criminal prosecution for structuring. A spokesman for the U.S. Attorney's Office declined further comment. The IRS did not respond to a request for comment on the case.

The Institute for Justice argues that the subpoena is an attempt to retroactively justify an improper seizure and punish the Vocaturas for not rolling over.

"At this point, the government is in so deep, they've put these guys through three years of hell—and held onto their money for three years—and so they feel like they need to justify it," said Robert Everett Johnson, an attorney for the Institute for Justice who is representing the Vocaturas. "So

132

now they're going to conduct this investigation into the bakery in some effort to try to find something that will make it look like they were doing the right thing all along."

The government's seizure of the Vocaturas' account is part of a broader pattern of concerns about the use of civil asset forfeiture, a practice that brings in billions of dollars each year to federal, state and local law enforcement agencies.

Critics say each step of the process is ripe for abuse. Authorities frequently base seizures on weak circumstantial evidence. In some of the most publicized civil asset forfeiture cases, the mere presence of cash has constituted enough probable cause to justify a seizure. In cases like the Vocaturas', the act of depositing cash isn't necessarily illegal on its own, but authorities are quick to treat anyone who does it like a criminal.

Once the government seizes property, it's difficult to get back. Unlike in criminal trials, where suspects are considered innocent until proven guilty, property owners must often prove their innocence in civil forfeiture cases.

And those legal proceedings often become a battle of pocketbooks and willpower. Many people can't afford representation — especially if they are small business owners who are unable to tap into the very finances seized by the agency they're fighting. Many people choose not to contest the seizures. Others eventually give up, worn down by well-equipped prosecutors.

Once someone's assets are forfeited, those proceeds go to the agency that made the seizure — and there is very little oversight of how that money can be used. Critics of civil asset forfeiture say this dynamic incentivizes law enforcement officials to bring in as much money as possible, creating a motive to "police for profit" rather than for public interest or safety.

The IRS has used structuring allegations to seize hundreds of millions of dollars through civil asset forfeiture in recent years, some of which has been funneled directly into the agency's coffers. A report from the Institute for Justice put the total value of forfeitures—money the government kept in IRS structuring cases—at nearly $125 million between 2006 and 2013.

Of the more than 2,500 seizures in the report, at least one-third involved no claims of criminal activity beyond the cash transactions themselves. Only 1 in 5 were ultimately prosecuted as a criminal structuring case. The numbers also show that the IRS failed to keep seized money in many cases, which could be a troubling sign of over-prosecution.

The Vocaturas' home state of Connecticut is a hotbed for structuring-based seizures, according to IRS data provided to the Institute for Justice through a public records request. Among states with a single U.S. attorney, Connecticut ranks third worst for these sorts of seizures. Between 2005 and 2013, federal prosecutors in the state approved 9.2 seizures for suspected structuring for every 10,000 businesses in the state—a rate that the Institute for Justice says is dramatically higher than other states. to the Politics email.

How will Trump's administration impact you?

Civil forfeiture has long been an issue among activists who see it as a violation of property owners' rights. But criticism of its use in structuring cases briefly entered mainstream discussion following an October 2014 New York Times story on Carole Hinders, a 67-year-old Iowa restaurateur battling the IRS over $33,000 seized in response to allegations of structured payments. Like the Vocaturas, she said she was unaware of the law, and had been keeping her deposits under $10,000 to save the bank the extra paperwork.

The scrutiny surrounding Hinders' case and others led the IRS to announce last year that it would limit structuring seizures to individuals believed to be involved in other illegal activity. The agency said the adjustment would not be retroactive—meaning the change wouldn't necessarily apply to the Vocaturas, whose assets were already in IRS possession.

The Department of Justice followed suit in 2015, saying it would restrict "seizures for structuring until after a defendant has been criminally charged or has been found to have engaged in additional criminal activity, in most cases."

Months after the Times article, the IRS reluctantly agreed to give Hinders all of her money back. Most victims aren't so lucky, even in cases in which they successfully challenge a seizure.

Despite that policy change, the IRS continued to pursue forfeiture actions against the Vocaturas and other small business owners — even as the agency lost in court. In 2015, North Carolina convenience store owner Lyndon McLellan and the Institute for Justice triumphed over the federal government, winning back the more than $100,000 the IRS had seized from his bank account over allegations of structuring.

While similar cases played out in the media, David Vocatura says the government kept them in limbo as it waited for the news cycle to blow over.

"We thought with everything going on with structuring in the news that some judge or court would see that this is wrong and they shouldn't be doing this to us," he said.

In February, 33 months after the bakery's bank account was seized, Jongbloed broke his silence. He offered the Vocaturas an opportunity to end their ordeal, while also preventing the public backlash that had impeded recent structuring cases.

Though the federal government had still not filed criminal charges against the brothers, Jongbloed wanted them to plead guilty to structuring, a felony, and admit that they'd "acted with the intent to evade the reporting requirement."

By doing so, the Vocaturas would be subject to a potential four-year prison sentence and would have to agree to forfeit both the initial $68,000 and an additional $160,000 in personal assets between them.

But by getting the Vocaturas to admit guilt, the IRS would also have been able to keep the brothers from speaking out about their case. The plea deal would have served as an admission that the government had some cause to take their money. Nobody could accuse the government of once again abusing civil forfeiture if the victims ultimately handed over the money as punishment for a crime they had copped to.

Jongbloed noted that sanctions could be harsher if the case went to trial, and encouraged the Vocaturas to take the deal. The brothers, who still insist that they've done nothing wrong, rejected that offer.

On May 10, Jongbloed responded by demanding more than six years of business records documenting all of the bakery's dealings. He finally wants to figure out if the Vocaturas had actually broken the law when IRS agents raided their account.

But Johnson questions the timing of the request, and says it amounts to a retributive fishing expedition that will subject the Vocaturas to unfair scrutiny: "If you're an IRS investigator and you feel like you have to make a case against somebody because you have to justify what you've been doing to them, you start looking for any kind of ambiguity in their records, where you can claim, even if it's not true, that they're hiding income or not paying all of their taxes."

The Institute for Justice is now considering a motion to quash the subpoena.

"I didn't know what structuring was that day, until the agent explained to me what it was.... We're good, hardworking people and we run a clean, legitimate business."

While the government is finally giving the Vocaturas their money back, the fact that they were able to hold it for so long without taking concrete action shows how much leeway they have in these cases.

As long as the current system of civil asset forfeiture remains intact, new federal guidelines or policy are unlikely to be effective, said Steven L. Kessler, a New York attorney who has defended a number of clients in high-profile forfeiture cases. He believes clear legislative action is needed to keep the government from compromising people's property rights in the hunt for money.

"When the government says they're going to do that on their own, they're going to make the change, everyone is very happy and we move on to the next story," said Kessler. "Rarely does anything change, because we're dealing with a guideline—we're dealing with something that is within the full discretion of the government."

There are some rumblings in Congress for a legal overhaul.

Last week, Rep. Jim Sensenbrenner (R-Wis.) and a bipartisan group of co-sponsors introduced a bill to rein in civil asset forfeiture. Among the most significant measures, the Deterring Undue Enforcement by Protecting Rights of Citizens from Excessive Searches and Seizures Act of 2016, or the Due Process Act, would shift the burden of proof from the property owner to the government, and raise the standard needed to validate a forfeiture. If passed, the new law would require the government to provide "clear and convincing" evidence that property was substantially connected to criminal activity—still below the "beyond a reasonable doubt" standard for criminal convictions.

The bill would also give property owners a variety of tools to make it easier to contest a seizure, including quicker notice of the government's forfeiture motion, increased time to respond and a mechanism for property owners to recover attorney's fees in certain cases that end in a settlement.

Another piece of legislation proposed this week would specifically address civil forfeiture in structuring cases. The bill would officially put previously announced IRS and

Department of Justice policy changes into law, offering stronger protections for small business owners accused of nothing more than making cash deposits in amounts under $10,000.

These legislative fixes would do little for Vocatura's Bakery, however.

While their legal saga began as a civil forfeiture case, the IRS has now decided to pursue criminal forfeiture against them. That isn't addressed in the Due Process Act, which only deals with civil cases.

Nor is it assumed that these bills will pass. Civil asset forfeiture reform has hit snags in Congress before, in part due to aggressive lobbying from law enforcement groups intent on preserving the practice.

On Wednesday, the House Committee on Ways and Means is set to hold a hearing on "Protecting Small Business from IRS Abuse." The committee held a similar hearing in February 2015, in which IRS Commissioner John Koskinen admitted that the government's forfeiture case against McLellan, the North Carolina convenience store owner, was "not following" the agency's own policy.

Koskinen is set to give testimony again this week. Johnson is on the witness list as well, along with Institute for Justice clients who had their assets seized by the IRS in structuring cases.

Johnson says the Vocaturas' case should serve as further proof that the IRS is still using structuring laws to manipulate the legal process and unfairly target small businesses.

"The way you would expect the criminal justice system to work if you were reading your high school civics textbook is that you'd expect the government first to investigate people, then to obtain an indictment if they think something wrong has happened, and then to obtain a conviction and then finally to punish them," he said.

"But in this case that all has happened exactly backwards," Johnson continued. "The government first *punished the Vocaturas by taking their property, then they tried to get them to plead guilty to charges, and only when they refused to plead guilty did the government investigate.*"[7]

The business operations of a drug dealer or a terrorist have little in common with a Maryland dairy farmer. But, in a bizarre business tale, the IRS, in February 2012, seized nearly $63,000 from a pair of dairy farmers after a series of cash deposits came under scrutiny due to federal laws. Those rules were intended to target criminals, including money launderers, who deposit large amounts of cash in increments of less than $10,000 to evade authorities.

> *In a prior settlement with the government, Randy and Karen Sowers, who own South Mountain Creamery in Middletown, Maryland, got back a portion of the seized money, around $33,500. Now in a new letter filed this week to the Justice Department, a nonprofit organization that has been working with the farmers is helping in the fight to get back the rest of the couple's money—$29,500—despite the prior settlement.*
>
> *"We know the right thing to do would be to give this money back," says Robert Everett Johnson, an attorney at the Institute for Justice public interest law firm.*
>
> *Randy Sowers said his bank teller initially suggested that his wife keep deposits under $10,000 to avoid time-consuming paperwork at the bank. "We thought it was very legitimate," he said. Karen Sowers initially wanted to deposit $12,000 earned from a weekend farmer's market. "If I wanted to hide it, I would have put it in a can. We have trouble paying our bills and don't need the government coming and taking money from us."*
>
> *Despite settling previously with the government, the Sowerses and Johnson say they are owed all of the assets, and initially had to settle for fear of losing the full amount seized and potentially more assets.*
>
> *The IRS and Justice Department work closely together on these seizure-related cases.*

"Federal law prohibits the IRS from discussing specific taxpayers," IRS spokesman Dean Patterson told CNBC by email. A Justice Department spokesman also declined comment on specific cases.

The Sowers case has attracted attention among small business owners, who argue time-consuming paperwork and regulations sometimes can be nonsensical.

There have since been some policy changes. The IRS, in October 2014, said it would restrict asset forfeitures to cases in which the property owner is suspected of criminal activity. And a policy directive from the Department of Justice issued last March says the asset forfeiture program will focus on the "most serious illegal banking transactions."

While the policy shifts are meant to apply toward future cases and don't necessarily apply to those impacted in the past, the development hasn't stopped the Institute for Justice or business owners from fighting for their cash.

Congress has even gotten into the fray. The House Ways and Means Subcommittee on Oversight took up the Sowers case, and asked the Treasury Department to review similar cases.

The related cases include Khalid "Ken" Quran, who owns a convenience store in Greenville, North Carolina. He had more than $150,000 seized in June 2014 after he unknowingly agreed to forfeit his bank account when IRS agents visited his store, accusing him of skirting reporting laws. Quran denies the charges.

"He said, 'You need to sign a paper,' and I told him my English is not right," said Quran, an immigrant from the Middle East. "Then he read it to me like you would read the newspaper and said you need to sign it." Quran said he did nothing wrong. "No bank told me that. No bookkeeper told me that," he said.

He has not received any of his money back, and the Institute for Justice has also filed a petition on Quran's behalf. On Tuesday, the legal nonprofit sends a letter to the IRS, asking for his petition to be reviewed.

The law to target large cash deposits "was passed to target drug dealers, money launderers and hardened criminals, but, unfortunately, it's being applied to people who are guilty of doing nothing more than business in cash," said Johnson.[8]

In *The New York Times* articles that follow, the IRS seizes a business's funds. Then, it makes threats, claiming that making the case public would just "ratchet up the feelings in the agency."

Under mounting pressure, the Internal Revenue Service and the Justice Department have announced in recent months that they will no longer use a law designed to go after drug dealers and terrorists to seize the bank accounts of small business owners who are not suspected of criminal activity. But Lyndon McLellan, the owner of a convenience store in rural Fairmont, N.C., where catfish sandwiches go for $2.75, is still trying to recover the $107,702.66 — his entire business bank account — that was seized by the I.R.S. last summer.

Under the increasingly unpopular practice of civil forfeiture, law enforcement agents can seize property suspected of having ties to crime, even if no charges are filed — and then begin forfeiture proceedings, in which the burden of proof is on the owner. Often the cost of fighting such a seizure is greater than the value of the assets seized, and law enforcement agencies get to keep forfeiture proceeds. Such a windfall, critics say, creates perverse incentives, and the lack of due process runs counter to the central tenets of the American justice system.

Mr. McLellan's money was seized under a subset of civil forfeiture law that governs cash deposits under $10,000, the threshold at which a bank is required to report the transaction to the government. But limiting deposits to less than $10,000 to evade the reporting requirement, known as structuring, is illegal in its own right. Structuring seizures have ballooned in recent years as law enforcement task forces comb through hundreds of thousands of bank reports, often using warrants based on nothing more than a pattern of deposits. The I.R.S. alone made 639 structuring seizures in 2012, up from 114 in 2005.

The seizure dragnet has ensnared small business owners who operate with cash and may have legitimate reasons to keep their deposits low, or do not know that doing so could get them into trouble.

After these cases and others received public scrutiny, the I.R.S. announced last October that it would no longer pursue structuring cases unless the money was tied to some other illegal activity. The Justice Department followed suit in March. But neither change in policy was retroactive, and the United States attorney for the Eastern District of North Carolina has continued to pursue the forfeiture of Mr. McLellan's money, though no crime has been charged. The Justice Department declined to comment on an open case.

"It was like I was just slapped in the face with something. I didn't know what was going on," said Mr. McLellan, 50, who has a 10th-grade education and has built a small gas station into a convenience store and restaurant. "You work for something for 13, 14 years, and they take it in 13, 14 minutes."

During a Congressional hearing in February, Representative George Holding, a Republican from North Carolina, referred to Mr. McLellan's case, saying no crime other than structuring had been alleged. "If that case exists, then it's not following the policy," John Koskinen, the commissioner of the I.R.S., said.

But the prosecutor on the case, Steve West, was unmoved. Notified of the hearing by Mr. McLellan's lawyer at the time, he responded with concern that the seizure warrant in the case, filed under seal but later given to Mr. McLellan, had been handed over to a congressional committee, according to an email exchange provided to The

New York Times *by the Institute for Justice, a libertarian public interest law firm that has taken over the case.*

"Your client needs to resolve this or litigate it," Mr. West wrote. "But publicity about it doesn't help. It just ratchets up feelings in the agency." He concluded with a settlement offer in which the government would keep half the money.

Mr. McLellan's new lawyer, Robert Everett Johnson, said the fact that prosecutors refuse to drop the case shows that self-restraint by federal agencies is not enough and that Congress needs to rein in civil forfeiture. Republicans, led by Senators Rand Paul of Kentucky and Mike Lee of Utah, have filed a bill in the House and Senate to change the practice, and the Judiciary Committees of both houses are working on a proposal.[9]

For almost 40 years, Carole Hinders has dished out Mexican specialties at her modest cash-only restaurant. For just as long, she deposited the earnings at a small bank branch a block away—until last year, when two tax agents knocked on her door and informed her that they had seized her checking account, almost $33,000.

The Internal Revenue Service agents did not accuse Ms. Hinders of money laundering or cheating on her taxes—in fact, she has not been charged with any crime. Instead, the money was seized solely because she had deposited less than $10,000 at a time, which they viewed as an attempt to avoid triggering a required government report.

"How can this happen?" Ms. Hinders said in a recent interview. "Who takes your money before they prove that you've done anything wrong with it?"

The federal government does.

Using a law designed to catch drug traffickers, racketeers and terrorists by tracking their cash, the government has gone after run-of-the-mill business owners and wage earners without so much as an allegation that they

143

have committed serious crimes. The government can take the money without ever filing a criminal complaint, and the owners are left to prove they are innocent. Many give up.

"They're going after people who are really not criminals," said David Smith, a former federal prosecutor who is now a forfeiture expert and lawyer in Virginia. "They're middle-class citizens who have never had any trouble with the law."

On Thursday, in response to questions from The New York Times, the I.R.S. announced that it would curtail the practice, focusing instead on cases where the money is believed to have been acquired illegally or seizure is deemed justified by "exceptional circumstances."

Richard Weber, the chief of Criminal Investigation at the I.R.S., said in a written statement "This policy update will ensure that C.I. continues to focus our limited investigative resources on identifying and investigating violations within our jurisdiction that closely align with C.I.'s mission and key priorities." He added that making deposits under $10,000 to evade reporting requirements, called structuring, is still a crime whether the money is from legal or illegal sources. The new policy will not apply to past seizures.

The I.R.S. is one of several federal agencies that pursue such cases and then refer them to the Justice Department. The Justice Department does not track the total number of cases pursued, the amount of money seized or how many of the cases were related to other crimes, said Peter Carr, a spokesman.

But the Institute for Justice a Washington-based public interest law firm that is seeking to reform civil forfeiture practices, analyzed structuring data from the I.R.S., which made 639 seizures in 2012, up from 114 in 2005. Only one in five was prosecuted as a criminal structuring case.[10]

According to the statement surrounding the above case, the IRS still considers any deposits made under $10,000 to be subject to "illegal" structuring and makes no mention of any due process under a warrant or by a federal judge, but, instead, by an IRS director of field operations (DFO).

This is the full statement from the chief of Criminal Investigation of the Internal Revenue Service to *The New York Times Magazine* regarding the agency's policy on structuring cases:

> After a thorough review of our structuring cases over the last year and in order to provide consistency throughout the country (between our field offices and the U.S. attorney offices) regarding our policies, I.R.S.-C.I. will no longer pursue the seizure and forfeiture of funds associated solely with "legal source" structuring cases unless there are exceptional circumstances justifying the seizure and forfeiture and the case has been approved at the director of field operations (D.F.O.) level.
>
> While the act of structuring—whether the funds are from a legal or illegal source—is against the law, I.R.S.-C.I. special agents will use this act as an indicator that further illegal activity may be occurring. This policy update will ensure that C.I. continues to focus our limited investigative resources on identifying and investigating violations within our jurisdiction that closely align with C.I.'s mission and key priorities. The policy involving seizure and forfeiture in "illegal source" structuring cases will remain the same.[11]

I will refer you back to my claim that that the progressive income tax and the subsequent tax code enacted by each Congress since its inception has completely abandoned the Bill of Rights and due process.

Essentially, the IRS has the ability to steal your money under suspicion (even without supporting evidence) and keep it. You are guilty first, then have to prove your innocence and spend your life and money fighting them to get it back. Or worse: you're threatened with prison unless you plead guilty and allow them to keep it.

The practice has swept up dairy farmers in Maryland, an Army sergeant in Virginia saving for his children's college

145

education, and Ms. Hinders, 67, who has borrowed money, strained her credit cards, and taken out a second mortgage to keep her restaurant going.

Their money was seized under an increasingly controversial area of law known as civil asset forfeiture, which allows law enforcement agents to take property they suspect of being tied to crime even if no criminal charges are filed. Law enforcement agencies get to keep a share of whatever is forfeited.

Critics say this incentive has led to the creation of a law enforcement dragnet, with more than 100 multiagency task forces combing through bank reports, looking for accounts to seize. Under the Bank Secrecy Act, banks and other financial institutions must report cash deposits greater than $10,000. But since many criminals are aware of that requirement, banks also are supposed to report any suspicious transactions, including deposit patterns below $10,000. Last year, banks filed more than 700,000 suspicious activity reports. Owners, who are caught up in structuring cases, often cannot afford to fight. The median amount seized by the IRS was $34,000, according to the Institute for Justice analysis, while legal costs can easily mount to $20,000 or more.

There is nothing illegal about depositing less than $10,000 cash unless it is done specifically to evade the reporting requirement. But often a mere bank statement is enough for investigators to obtain a seizure warrant. In one Long Island case, the police submitted almost a year's worth of daily deposits by a business, ranging from $5,550 to $9,910. The officer wrote in his warrant affidavit that based on his training and experience, the pattern "is consistent with structuring." The government seized $447,000 from the business, a cash-intensive candy and cigarette distributor that has been run by one family for 27 years.

There are often legitimate business reasons for keeping deposits below $10,000, said Larry Salzman, a lawyer with the Institute for Justice who is representing Ms. Hinders and the Long Island family pro bono. For example, he said, a grocery store owner in Fraser, Mich., had an insurance policy that covered only up to $10,000 cash. When he neared the limit, he would make a deposit.

Ms. Hinders said that she did not know about the reporting requirement and that for decades, she thought she had been doing everyone a favor.

"My mom had told me if you keep your deposits under $10,000, the bank avoids paperwork," she said. "I didn't actually think it had anything to do with the IRS."

To date, the Due Process Act which was introduced in 2017 never made it out of committee. The act of civil forfeiture can be effective in fighting crimes, wherein a conviction has occurred. Seizing assets (including cash) under suspicion is completely Anti-American and is not Constitutional. Additionally, the hordes of assets seized by various government agencies can be a windfall for the local county sheriff's department as well as the IRS.

Rep. Jim Sensenbrenner (R-Wis.) introduced legislation Wednesday that would reform federal civil asset forfeiture laws, offering key protections to innocent people whose property is seized by the government. The Deterring Undue Enforcement by Protecting Rights of Citizens from Excessive Searches and Seizures Act (H.R. 5283), or Due Process Act, is the most significant, if not first, major reform of federal forfeiture laws since 2000, when Congress passed the Civil Asset Forfeiture Reform Act.

Civil asset forfeiture is a legal tool by which law enforcement agencies seize either tangible property or cash without ever arresting or charging, let alone convicting, someone of a crime. In federal forfeiture proceedings, the government can permanently seize the property or cash based on a low standard of evidence—a preponderance of the evidence, or a 51 percent likelihood that the information presented is true—and, in a perversion of justice, the burden of proof falls on the property owner. A legal fiction exists in forfeiture proceedings because the case is brought

147

against the seized item, not an individual. The property owner bears the full cost of all legal fees, even if they cannot afford counsel, and is responsible for navigating the complicated and onerous process.

Previous efforts to reform federal civil asset forfeiture laws fell far short of offering meaningful protections to innocent property owners. In 2000, then-House Judiciary Committee Chairman Henry Hyde (R-Ill.) introduced the Civil Asset Forfeiture Reform Act, or CAFRA. As originally introduced, the bill would have raised the standard of evidence to "clear and convincing," the highest in civil court. Unfortunately, it was watered down during the legislative process, making the effort a missed opportunity. The value of seizures that were subjected to federal forfeiture subsequently exploded, from $313 million in 2000 to more than $1 billion in 2013.[12]

The Internal Revenue Service (IRS) has a long, well-documented history of abusing federal forfeiture laws. They seize assets from innocent Americans on the mere suspicion of malfeasance. If the IRS believes a citizen is structuring deposits to avoid reporting requirements, the agency can seize your money. Administrative reforms were made in 2015 to roll back some abuses, but there is still much work to be done.

People like dairy farmer Randy Sowers, who had $30,000 wrongfully seized from him and his family, can see their lives change almost instantly because of the IRS's wild speculations about their finances. Thankfully, the Sowers family had their money returned to them when it was determined the seizure was wrongful, but we can't count on every victim being so fortunate. A similar situation happened to Andrew Clyde, the owner of Clyde Armory in Athens, Georgia. The IRS seized $950,000 from him, eventually returning all but $50,000. Clyde spent roughly $150,000 in attorneys' fee.

According to the Institute for Justice, from 2005 to 2012, the IRS seized roughly $242 million in assets across 2,500 cases for offenses that were only alleged at that point. Frighteningly, in about one-third of those cases, the "offense" was making a series of transactions below $10,000. The IRS is casting a wide net and is threatening to catch scores of innocent families in it.

The broad, irresponsible nature of this practice was brought to light through a report done by the Treasury Inspector General for Tax Administration (TIGTA). TIGTA took a sample of 278 seizure cases and found that in a whopping 91 percent of them, there was no evidence that the funds were a part of illegal structuring or otherwise illegal activity. This is outright theft propagated against American citizens.[12]

Senator Rand Paul (the Fair Act) and others in Congress, in their attempt to change the due process laws when it comes to asset seizures, have found subcommittees unwilling to tackle the issue for fear of "being soft on crime."

Although most of the asset forfeitures in the U.S. occur with the Drug Enforcement Agency, the Justice Department's Office of Inspector reported that $3.2 billion had been taken from Americans *never* charged with a crime![13]

In 2017, the Justice Department issued a directive for asset seizures that indicate federal jurisdiction over individual states that have laws that specifically ban these types of procedures without due process.

Maybe even more troubling is the indication in this policy directive (below) from Sessions' office that the asset owner can be notified up to forty-five days later—*imagine your cash is gone and you have to wait forty-five days to get a notice telling you who took it*—and there is no mention of any neutral judge or magistrate involved in the process!

Here is another place where the U.S. Constitution is completely shredded, and Liberty has died. Assets forfeitures are not exclusive to the IRS, but it is a very useful and abusive tool at their disposal, one which they obviously use to a significant degree.

U.S. Department of Justice

Criminal Division

Money Laundering and Asset Recovery Section   *Washington, D.C. 20530*

POLICY DIRECTIVE 17-1

TO: Heads of Department of Justice Components
                   United States Attorneys
                   Participants in the Department of Justice Asset Forfeiture Program

FROM: Deborah Connor, Acting Chief *Deborah Connor by MCD*
                   Money Laundering and Asset Recovery Section
                   Criminal Division

SUBJECT: Policy Guidance on the Attorney General's Order on Federal Adoption and
                   Forfeiture of Property Seized by State and Local Law Enforcement Agencies

On July 19, 2017, the Attorney General issued an Order allowing Department of Justice components and agencies to forfeit assets seized by state or local law enforcement (referred to in the order as "federal adoptions"). Under the Attorney General's Order, federal adoption of all types of assets seized lawfully by state or local law enforcement under their respective state laws is authorized whenever the conduct giving rise to the seizure violates federal law. The net equity and value thresholds found in the Department of Justice *Asset Forfeiture Policy Manual* will continue to apply.[1] Agencies and components should prioritize the adoption of assets that will advance the Attorney General's Violent Crime Reduction Strategy.

The Department, through legal counsel for federal investigative agencies as well as through the U.S. Attorneys' Offices, will continue to ensure that adoptions are conducted in compliance with law and Department policies. Specifically, the following safeguards, among others, shall be maintained and implemented to ensure that there is sufficient evidence of criminal activity and that the evidence is well documented:

- To ensure that adoptions involve property lawfully seized, legal counsel at the
  federal agency adopting the seized property must continue to review all seizures

---

[1] *See Asset Forfeiture Policy Manual* (2016), Chap. 1, Sec. I.D.1, establishing minimum net equity thresholds of at least $5,000 for vehicles, and a minimum amount of $5,000 for cash seizures, or at least $1,000 if the person from whom the cash was seized either was, or is, being criminally prosecuted by state or federal authorities for criminal activities related to the property. U.S. Attorneys' Offices, in consultation with local federal law enforcement agencies, may continue to establish higher thresholds for judicial forfeiture cases in order to best address the crime threat in individual judicial districts.

for compliance with law, especially seizures made pursuant to an exception to the Fourth Amendment's warrant requirement.

- To assist federal legal counsel in this review process, the form used by state and local agencies seeking federal adoption of seized assets, *Request for Adoption of State and Local Seizure* ("adoption form"), will require that the state or local agency provide additional information about the probable cause determination justifying the seizure. This additional information in the adoption form will better document probable cause in the first instance, and provide federal legal counsel with the relevant information relating to probable cause for review. State and local agencies will also be required to certify on the form that they have obtained a turnover order, if necessary.

- Adoptions of cash in amounts equal to or less than $10,000 may require additional safeguards. Those adoptions will be permissible where the seizure was conducted: (1) pursuant to a state warrant, (2) incident to arrest for an offense relevant to the forfeiture, (3) at the same time as a seizure of contraband relevant to the forfeiture, or (4) where the owner or person from whom the property is seized makes admissions regarding the criminally derived nature of the property. If a federal agency seeks to adopt cash equal to or less than $10,000 and none of these safeguards is present, then the agency may proceed with the adoption only if the U.S. Attorney's Office first concurs.

- Department officials should proceed with particular caution when deciding whether to waive the Department's net equity thresholds for real property, *see Policy Manual: Asset Forfeiture Policy* (2016), Chap. 13, Sec. I.B, and in considering the forfeiture of personal residences where title or ownership lies with persons not implicated in illegal conduct. *See id.* at Chap. 2, Sec. VIII.C.

In order to give individual property owners an opportunity to challenge the seizure as soon as practicable, the Department will expedite federal agencies' decisions regarding adoptions and their provision of notice to interested parties. State and local law enforcement agencies must request federal adoption within 15 calendar days following the date of seizure. The adopting federal agency must send notice to interested parties within 45 days of the date of seizure. These time limitations may be extended for good cause by the supervisory forfeiture counsel (or higher-level official) of the adopting agency, provided that such extensions are documented in writing and include a description of the circumstances justifying the extension. Any such extensions remain subject to statutory time limits pursuant to 18 U.S.C. § 983(a)(1)(A)(iv).

To facilitate implementation of these safeguards and help ensure that federal adoptions advance federal law enforcement objectives,[2] the Department is enhancing its asset forfeiture

---

[2] This change in Department policy does not affect the ability of state and local agencies to pursue the forfeiture of assets pursuant to their respective state laws. Moreover, when a state or local agency has seized property as part of an ongoing state criminal investigation and the criminal defendants are being prosecuted in state court, any forfeiture action should generally be pursued in state court assuming that state law authorizes the forfeiture. *See Asset Forfeiture Policy Manual* (2016), Chap. 14, Sec. I.

training. Beginning in 2018, law enforcement agencies participating in the Department of Justice Asset Forfeiture Program must provide annual training on state and federal laws related to asset forfeiture to their law enforcement officers. Specialized course material for state and local law enforcement will be available later this year.

This policy is effective immediately and applies prospectively to all new requests for adoption by state and local law enforcement. The Order and this policy guidance supersede all inconsistent adoption policy and procedures in any Department of Justice publication, including the U.S. Attorney's Manual § 9-116.000 *et seq.*; the *Attorney General's Guidelines to Seized and Forfeited Property* (2005); the *Asset Forfeiture Policy Manual* (2016), Chapter 14; and the *Guide to Equitable Sharing for State and Local Law Enforcement Agencies* (2009), Sections III.B and III.B.2. In particular, the Order supersedes Attorney General Order Nos. 3485-2015 and 3488-2015, "Prohibition on Certain Federal Adoptions of Seizures by State and Local Law Enforcement Agencies" (Jan. 12 and 16, 2015). This policy directive supersedes Policy Directive 15-1, "Policy Limiting the Federal Adoptions of Seizures by State and Local Law Enforcement Agencies" (Jan. 16, 2015); and Policy Directive 15-2, "Additional Guidance on the Policy Limiting the Federal Adoption of Seizures by State and Local Law Enforcement Agencies" (Feb. 10, 2015). Accordingly, the *Determination of Sufficient Federal Involvement for an Asset Seized by State or Local Law Enforcement* form is no longer required.

The adoption form will be updated to reflect these policy changes. The Department also will make conforming updates to the Consolidated Asset Tracking System (CATS). Until the CATS update is complete, agencies must manually track this information so that it is available for subsequent submission and review.

Consistent with current policy, state and local agencies are required to complete the adoption form only when seeking federal adoptions. Seizures made as part of joint federal-state investigations or pursuant to federal seizure warrants are not considered adoptions. Agency participants must review the circumstances of a seizure by state and local law enforcement to determine whether it is a federal adoption.

If you have questions regarding this policy directive or the application of the Attorney General's Order, please contact the Money Laundering and Asset Recovery Section at (202) 514-1263.

With an 80 percent conviction rate in criminal tax cases, this means that a full 20 percent who were found not guilty in those cases could have been subject to asset seizures by the IRS. Per the IRS table below, nearly 12,000 criminal tax investigations occurred during 2014–2016, meaning 2,400 who were found *not guilty* may have had their assets seized upon *suspicion* of a crime.

Statistical data from the IRS itself also shows a robust criminal investigation (CI) in criminal tax prosecutions, with 80 percent conviction rates: [14]

	FY 2016	FY 2015	FY 2014
Investigations Initiated	3395	3853	4297
Prosecution Recommendations	2744	3289	3478
Informations/Indictments	2761	3208	3272
Convictions	2672	2879	3110
Sentenced*	2699	3092	3268
Percent to Prison	79.9%	80.8%	79.6%

*Sentence includes confinement to federal prison, halfway house, home detention, or some combination thereof.

A fiscal year runs from October 1 through September 30.

Data Source: Criminal Investigation Management Information System

Is this still America?

Lenin and Stalin would be proud. The progressive income tax system invokes fear and intimidation. Constitutional and God-given rights are systematically stripped from the citizenry. We are guilty until proven innocent. There is absolutely nothing admirable, neutral, or bipartisan about the Internal Revenue Service.

13

★

PUNISH THINE ENEMIES

"I want to be clear that no matter how you say it—whether it's suspended, eliminated or ended—the IRS stopped this practice long ago and is committed to never using such a list or process ever again."

—IRS Commissioner John Koskinen
2016 Statement on IRS Targeting of Conservative & Tea Party Groups

I f you were going to design a weapon that would confound your enemies, how would you create it?

Maybe you would make it the type of weapon that is so massive, intricate, convoluted, and arbitrary that you could force it upon your enemies simply because its sheer volume and complexity would be something they could neither fully understand nor come to any common conclusions as to its operation....

Maybe you would equip the blunt end of this weapon or the tip of its spear with the ability to destroy your enemies' lives by taking everything they own and rendering them penniless and powerless to respond....

Maybe, you would design such a weapon where laws, if such existed, were powerless to stop it.

Maybe you would design this weapon without regard for natural, God-given laws or the basic tenets that founded your country via a Constitution? After all, that document was likely written by old, white slaveholders....

155

Maybe, to make this new political weapon so effective, you would put it in the hands of a leviathan, Gestapo-style bureaucracy with unlimited and unchecked powers; one that doesn't bother with a warrant from a judge; one that has unfettered access to seize citizens' money and assets; one that can put its citizens in prison and facilitate political punishments without the statesmen in the Oval Office or Capitol Hill bothering to get themselves dirty.

While you're at it, develop the ideal mechanism for Congress to vote themselves into enough of the Treasury so as to assure their reelection, and maintain their power by championing social justice, welfare, and income redistribution — and by punishing the evil rich.

After all, this grand design is the perfect weapon. It was designed by Karl Marx, and it's called the progressive income tax!

Elliott Roosevelt, son of President Franklin D. Roosevelt, claims FDR was the first president to use the progressive income tax and its IRS enforcement powers as a weapon:

> "My Father," Elliott Roosevelt observed of his famous parent, "may have been the originator of the concept of employing the IRS as a weapon of political retribution." Not until Franklin D. Roosevelt's presidency had the federal government taken so much individual income. In 1935, when Roosevelt hiked the top marginal income tax rate to 79 percent and the top marginal estate tax rate to 70 percent, millionaires searched for deductions and loopholes to protect their private property. During the 1930s, FDR began experimenting with the Bureau of Internal Revenue (later renamed the Internal Revenue Service or IRS), which had earlier been placed under the Treasury Department, as a means of attacking political enemies and generating more revenue for his New Deal programs.[1]

It was a well-known secret in Washington, D.C. and in Baton Rouge, Louisiana that Governor Hughey P. Long and FDR had a running feud. FDR made sure his Treasury secretary kept the IRS busy on Long's heels and eventually was able to use that "heat" to manipulate his family members so they'd endorse FDR long after Hughey's assassination.

FDR's use of the IRS's power was the first time a president had brazenly used this newfound weapon so successfully — and so often.

FDR's IRS targets included William Randolph Hearst, the newspaper mogul; famous Catholic radio personality Father Charles Coughlin; New Jersey crime boss "Nucky" Johnson; Atlantic City Mayor Frank Hague; Missouri Democrat Tom Pendergast; LBJ donor Brown & Root, Inc.; Andrew Mellon; and dozens of others.[1]

But FDR especially went after the wealthy:

> Wealthy Americans were a natural target for Roosevelt and the IRS. For one thing, rich people had the money that Roosevelt wanted to fund the WPA (Works Progress Administration) and other programs. His highly progressive tax rate secured some of this cash, but people with wealth quickly sought tax loopholes. The complexity of earning money, and then trying to shelter it legally, made rich Americans an obvious target for generating federal revenue. Another related consideration is that rich people were a nucleus of energy blowing against the New Deal. No one likes to pay taxes, and many wealthy Americans resented paying over half of their annual earnings for federal programs that they loathed. Working from January to July or August for Roosevelt and the rest of the year for themselves became a dreary prospect to face and they complained loudly.[1]

FDR even rewarded two of his IRS stooges by nominating them to the Supreme Court (Robert Jackson and Frank Murphy). This was, in part, because of their loyalty in going after political enemies through the progressive tax code.[1]

During President Eisenhower's administration, the FBI allegedly had unlimited access to confidential tax returns of political targets such as the John Birch Society, the NAACP, and the National Council of Churches. The organization formed under FBI Director J. Edgar Hoover (COINTELPRO) was used by Eisenhower to spy on domestic political rivals.[2]

President Kennedy was also no stranger to using the IRS and the progressive income tax code to target political enemies. His

Ideological Organizations Project was allegedly used to go after right-wing foundations and challenge their tax-exempt status. Kennedy's FBI carefully coordinated with the IRS in a domestic (and sometimes illegal) counterintelligence campaign, using COINTELPRO to surveil, infiltrate, and discredit such "subversives" as Martin Luther King, Jr. and the Southern Christian Leadership Conference, as well as Communist Party USA, the Nation of Islam, the Black Panthers, feminist organizations, and the Ku Klux Klan.

While many of those organizations may make someone's "list" regarding potentially subversive organizations, these actions don't speak well for American civil liberties. Many of these organizations were simply audited because they were on the JFK list to target. In addition, reports surfaced that popular tactics included withholding of evidence by federal agents, witness tampering, witness harassment, and even perjury.[3]

President Richard Nixon had an extensive internal "enemies list" he used to make life hell for his political rivals. He eventually had direct Articles of Impeachment levied against him during the Watergate Scandal, due to his attempts to use the IRS against enemies and many other actions:

Using the powers of the office of President of the United States, Richard M. Nixon, in violation of his constitutional oath faithfully to execute the office of President of the United States and, to the best of his ability, preserve, protect, and defend the Constitution of the United States, and in disregard of his constitutional duty to take care that the laws be faithfully executed, has repeatedly engaged in conduct violating the constitutional rights of citizens, impairing the due and proper administration of justice and the conduct of lawful inquiries, or contravening the laws governing agencies of the executive branch and the purposed of these agencies.

This conduct has included one or more of the following:

1. He has, acting personally and through his subordinates and agents, endeavored to obtain from

the Internal Revenue Service, in violation of the constitutional rights of citizens, confidential information contained in income tax returns for purposed not authorized by law, and to cause, in violation of the constitutional rights of citizens, income tax audits or other income tax investigations to be initiated or conducted in a discriminatory manner.[4]

During the Clinton administration, claims were made that political pressure was applied to the IRS so that conservative groups such as the Heritage Foundation, the National Rifle Association, and Judicial Watch were audited. Also, one of Clinton's sexual accusers, Paula Jones, was also audited, claiming the IRS official stated, "What do you expect when you sue the president?"[5]

Allegations were also made against President George W. Bush that he had singled out the NAACP and the environmental group Greenpeace for audits, although no proof of a direct correlation between those audits and his administration could be found. The problem with this type of system is the party that's not of the existing president's political affiliation could claim this type of scandal, and, based on history, it's hard not to argue that every president has used this vicious tool (since the Sixteenth Amendment was ratified) to wreak havoc on political enemies.

Thanks to today's nonstop news cycle, President Obama's (much more recent) IRS scandal was front and center for nearly three years. Congressional hearing after hearing saw the IRS march feckless government employees—such as Lois Lerner, IRS Commissioner John Koskinen, former Commissioners Steven T. Miller, Douglas Shulman, and others—to hearing after hearing.

President Obama's famous live interview with television commentator Bill O'Reilly showed how far Obama would go to cover up the political corruption that existed at the IRS:

O'REILLY: I've got to get to the IRS....
OBAMA: Yes.
O'REILLY: Because I don't know what happened there and I'm hoping maybe you can tell us. Douglas Shulman,

former IRS chief, he was cleared into the White House 157 times, more than any of your cabinet members, more than any other IRS guy in the history, by far. Okay, why was Douglas Shulman here 157 times? Why?

OBAMA: Mr. Shulman, as the head of the IRS, is constantly coming in, because at the time, we were trying to set up the, uh, HealthCare.gov and the IRS—

O'REILLY: What did he have to do with that?

OBAMA: And the IRS is involved in making sure that that works as part of the overall healthcare team.

O'REILLY: So it was all healthcare?

OBAMA: Number two, we've also got the IRS involved when it comes to some of the financial reforms to make sure that we don't have taxpayer-funded bailouts in the future. So you had all these different agendas in which the head of the IRS is naturally involved.

O'REILLY: Did you speak to him a lot—

OBAMA: [Inaudible.]

O'REILLY: —yourself?

OBAMA: I do not recall meeting with him in any of these meetings that are pretty routine meetings that we had.

O'REILLY: Okay, so you don't—you don't recall seeing Shulman, because what some people are saying is that the IRS was used—

OBAMA: Yes.

O'REILLY: —at a—at a local level in Cincinnati, and maybe other places to go after—

OBAMA: Absolutely wrong.

O'REILLY: —to go after—

OBAMA: Absolutely wrong.

O'REILLY: But how do you know that, because we—we still don't know what happened there?

OBAMA: Bill, we do—that's not what happened. They— folks have, again, had multiple hearings on this. I mean, these kinds of things keep on surfacing, in part because you and your TV station will promote them.

O'REILLY: But don't—

OBAMA: But when [inaudible].
O'REILLY: —think there are unanswered questions?
OBAMA: Bill, when you actually look at this stuff, there have been multiple hearings on it. What happened here was that you've got a—
O'REILLY: But there's no definition on it.
OBAMA: You've got a 501(c)(4) law that people think is focusing. No—that the folks did not know how to implement….
O'REILLY: Okay….
OBAMA: Because it basically says—
O'REILLY: So you're saying there was no—
OBAMA: —if you are involved—
O'REILLY: —no corruption there at all, none?
OBAMA: That's not what I'm saying.
O'REILLY: [Inaudible.]
OBAMA: That's actually—
O'REILLY: No, no, but I want to know what—
OBAMA: [Inaudible.]
O'REILLY: —you're saying. You're the leader of the country.
OBAMA: Absolutely.
O'REILLY: You're saying no corruption?
OBAMA: No.
O'REILLY: None? No?
OBAMA: There were some—there were some boneheaded decisions—
O'REILLY: Boneheaded decisions….
OBAMA: —out of—out of a local office.
O'REILLY: But no mass corruption?
OBAMA: Not even mass corruption, not even a smidgeon of corruption, I would say.

Not even a smidgeon of corruption, says Obama?

Despite the infamous *"not a smidgeon of corruption"* claim made that day in 2014 by Obama, in May of 2013, Obama had stated:

I've reviewed the Treasury Department watchdog's report, and the misconduct that it uncovered is inexcusable. It's inexcusable, and Americans are right to be angry about it, and I am angry about it. I will not tolerate this kind of behavior in any an agency, but especially in the IRS, given the power that it has and the reach that it has in all of our lives.[6]

Not even a smidgeon of corruption, says Obama....

The U.S. House of Representatives Committee on Oversight and Government Reform, chaired by Darrell Issa (R) from California, begged to differ.

The IRS tried to sidestep any potential firestorm by allowing Lois Lerner to admit this publicly at a nondescript conference, where she hoped nobody would pay attention and where the mea culpa would get little attention. Instead, the story steadily picked up news coverage until it began to roil the headlines.

The entire tax-exempt problem for Lerner and the IRS was prompted by their disdain for the *Citizens United v. FEC* ruling in the Supreme Court that essentially allowed corporations to have free speech rights, interpreted to mean expenditures on political campaigns could not be limited. The ramped rhetoric by the Democrats and the left made for a fertile environment for the IRS to discriminate in 501-c applications for conservative Tea Party groups to get approved.

Flagrant and pervasive management failures by Washington officials contributed substantially to the misconduct. When asked to answer questions about allegations of IRS targeting, these senior officials—including former Commissioner Doug Shulman and Exempt Organizations Director Lois Lerner—covered up the wrongdoing by providing incomplete and misleading information to Congress. Shulman specifically gave Congress "assurances" that the IRS was not targeting Tea Party groups, when he knew at that time that those groups had been identified using inappropriate criteria, that they had been subjected to excessive delays, and that they had been harassed with unnecessary and burdensome questions. Lerner, likewise, made several false statements to the Committee, and specifically defended before the committee the IRS's use of certain questions that the IRS had already identified internally as inappropriate.

The Committee's investigation highlights the unfortunate reality of the IRS. Because "the power to tax involves the power to destroy," American taxpayers expect the IRS to be neutral, independent, and apolitical. The modern-day IRS, however, with its vast authority, has violated these basic tenets. The IRS's outsized role in implementing Obamacare—a highly partisan law rammed through Congress without any meaningful bipartisan compromise—has fundamentally transformed the tax agency. Evidence shows an IRS responsive to the partisan policy objectives of the White House and an IRS leadership that coordinates with political appointees of the Obama administration.

The Committee's investigation has resulted in the following findings to date about the Internal Revenue Service's inappropriate treatment of tax-exempt applicants:

- The IRS targeted conservative-oriented applicants for tax-exempt status;
- Unlike applications from conservative groups, the small batch of applications from the liberal-oriented groups received additional scrutiny for non-political reasons. Of the applications that received additional scrutiny, only seven contained the word "progress" or "progressive," all of which were subsequently approved. By the IRS, while Tea Party groups were subjected to an unprecedented degree of review and years-long delays;
- Senior IRS officials covered up the misconduct and misled the Congress about the existence and nature of the targeting;

- The IRS sought to rein in conservative-oriented non-profits as early as 2010;
- The Administration is using the targeting as a pretext to support its proposed regulation to limit political speech of conservative non-profits;
- Mismanagement among the senior leadership of the IRS contributed to the targeting;
- The IRS and Obama Administration knowingly and wrongly blamed line-level employees for the misconduct;
- Employees of the IRS inappropriately used non-official email to conduct official government business;
- The IRS has compromised its traditional position as an independent tax administrator;
- The Obama Administration exhibited a lack of accountability for the IRS misconduct;
- Lois Lerner's refusal to testify hindered the Committee's investigation;
- The IRS obstructed the committee's investigation; and
- The White House and congressional Democrats obstructed the Committee's investigation.[6]

Soon after the news of the scandal heated up dramatically, Lerner's attorney claimed she would take the Fifth Amendment and not testify. To demonstrate the tone-deafness (or sheer bravado) of the agency, the IRS also announced Lerner would receive a $42,000 bonus, and IRS Commissioner Steven T. Miller would receive a $100,000 bonus shortly before his resignation. A total of $70 million in bonuses were slated for IRS employees during that year.[7]

Although the IRS fully expects you to document every line item of your tax return and keep those records for seven years, apparently, we cannot expect them to keep Lois Lerner's emails on their servers for at least the period of their standard archiving procedures. The IRS conveniently "lost" thousands of Lerner's emails and then did not report them missing to the congressional committees under oath until much later in the investigation. Apparently, Hillary Clinton and Lois Lerner have the same modus operandi when it comes to hiding emails.

The public became somewhat used to seeing the Obama administration in scandal hearings, between this IRS investigation, Operation Fast and Furious, Benghazi, and others. But, like with the others, Obama's FBI, under the direction of Attorney General Eric Holder, stated no criminal charges would be filed, despite Congress issuing charges against Lerner for contempt of Congress. The Justice Department advised (in October 2014) Congress that it was closing its investigation and would not recommend charges.

The public has gotten somewhat numb to all the investigative hearings. It would seem each subcommittee of each branch of government wanted to conduct their own investigation, especially since they could grandstand in front of the cameras. It would do them well for their next reelection for their base — or they thought it may bode well for them to run for the next higher office — even the White House.

When the public sees James Clapper, Lois Lerner, various IRS commissioners, and Donna Rice outright perjure themselves in front of Congress (and suffer no consequences whatsoever), it completely demoralizes the taxpaying American public. Maybe our Founders never figured the Executive Branch would be so corrupt, selectively disregarding their law enforcement powers to arrest and prosecute obvious lawbreakers.

Today, it's my prediction that, at some point, President Trump's personal and corporate tax returns will be leaked. There is no law that requires a president to disclose their tax returns, although most have done it. If I were Trump, I wouldn't disclose mine, either.

In a progressive tax system such as the one that exists in America today, the tax code is a fertile ground for rampant corruption. Nobody's tax returns are private or safe. Imagine the corruption we don't know about. How many times has the government used a tax return to leverage or curry favors or reward cronies?

And, worse, imagine ending up on the enemies list. We know, for example, Nixon and FDR had one, but who else? The truth of the matter is your political beliefs may expose you to *someone's* list—and that *someone* does not have to be sitting in the Oval Office to cause you great harm.

We have seen the machinations of the *Deep State* in the FBI and Department of Justice since Trump ran for, and has been elected, president. Could we be so naïve to think that it's not worse in the darkest corners of the IRS?

Trump maintains he will release his tax returns once his audits are over. For someone like Trump, with his many varied business interests, tax schedules, and real property, that may be *never*.

One thing I have learned: when the IRS identifies you as a target—whether political, ideological, or for the crime of working hard and owning a business—if they get their claws into you for an audit, it will likely only end when you have no more taxes to file. In other words, when you are dead. And, even then, your legacy to your spouse or children may be an audit with which they will have to deal.

As I've tried to do often throughout the book, please harken back to our Founders. Try to name a Founder (if you can) who would have put up with this type of tyranny from our *own* government, much less a foreign occupier?

Even the centralist of his day, Alexander Hamilton, stated: "It's not tyranny we desire; it's a just, limited, federal government."

14

★

AN ENEMY OF THE STATE

"The State can't give you freedom, and the State can't take it away. You're born with it like your eyes, like your ears. Freedom is something you assume, then you wait for someone to try to take it away. The degree to which you resist is the degree to which you are free."

—Utah Phillips
Western Folk Singer & Poet

Your local postal service person knocks on the door to give you a piece of certified mail. It's from the Internal Revenue Service.

Your heart stops momentarily. The postal worker hands you two large, thick, white envelopes. One is addressed to you, the other to your spouse. You smile weakly, shut the door, and sit down.

You open one envelope and see that the IRS is requesting documentation and you are officially under audit—with a designated time and place to appear with your records. The envelope that's for your spouse contains the exact same information.

Attached is a list of the documents under review. It's a very long list. Also attached is a pamphlet supposedly explaining what your rights are while under audit.

This is the moment of truth that every American taxpayer tries to avoid.

Now, try to imagine this same scenario playing out *every* year. Every. Single. Year. For years. And, no matter what you do, you can't escape the audits. You file the taxes yourself, you use a CPA, you change CPAs, you change entities, you hire a tax attorney...but the audits keep happening.

Some years, your tax professional has been paid much more money to handle your audits than the IRS ever gets out of you, the discrepancy is so small, minuscule.

My CPAs would try to reason with me, telling me I have several businesses and a few of them have Schedule C expenses, even recommending that I not take completely legitimate and legal deductions for things like home office and business travel expenses so as to "lower my audit scoring risk." To this day, none of my tax professionals have ever been able to show me this "supposed" scoring matrix that makes audits more likely. In fact, it's hard to get two tax professionals to agree on what these factors are.

The most knowledgeable source on tax issues I've ever found is top tax expert Robert G. Bernhoft, who was kind enough to write the Foreword in this book. We know certain criteria, amounts of income, deductions, and other factors contribute to the likelihood of audits. But, if a "matrix" or "recipe" does exist, it's a closely held secret, like the formula for Coca-Cola®.

I was audited "randomly" in 2002, 2004, and 2006. That was bad enough. When the audits started becoming repetitious in 2008, 2009, and 2010, I had had enough. Yet, they continued in 2012 and 2013. Coincidentally, my audits were beginning to align with the Obama years.

Between 2008 and 2010, I found myself on the "no-fly" list of some kind, trying to board a commercial aircraft for flights related to my businesses. I can't describe how embarrassing it feels when your boarding pass does not go through and you have to step aside to let everyone else board the aircraft, only to see it leave the gate without you. The poor gate agents can only tell you so much, giving you an 800 number at Homeland Security, where, if it does get answered by a live person, you sit on hold for an hour. To date, I have never been told why this happened.

During this time period, when the fight over Obamacare really heated up, the Tea Party was born. I became immersed in the Tea Party movement, going to meetings, organizing and reaching out to candidates and elected representatives statewide and nationwide. I did my best to bring others to the grassroots movement. Passing Obamacare's thousands of pages without reading the bill was incomprehensible to me, and I never forgave any elected representative for voting for it—no matter which party.

It was during this period—mad as hell and at the behest of my wife (who was concerned about my health due to the pent-up rage I went to bed with every night after watching *Fox News*®)—that I sat down in 2011 to pen my first political thriller, *Patriots of Treason*. I wrote my debut novel in a couple of months, seething at the place I'd found myself in, which was mired in receipts, tax forms, and minutia of unproductive retracing of financial steps from years prior.

Little did I know what the government had in store for me.

At first, writing *Patriots of Treason* was fun, therapeutic, a way to blow off steam. A few folks read it and told me I should send it to publishers, so I did. The next thing I knew, I had a small publishing deal from an independent publisher in Missouri. I don't think the publisher thought it would sell at the pace that it did. We were both pleasantly surprised beyond my imagination. The greatest thing about the book was the book tour, where I met many like-minded individuals.

That's all it took; I was bit by the writing bug and my next book was already in the planning stages. I found that my publisher was loath to promote the book at certain book events because she didn't want to be judged by the "*radical* conservative work of fiction" she'd published, and, maybe, she was a little embarrassed it had done as well as it had, too. *You would think she would be happy.* Later, when issued arose of royalties, that was all I needed. Like many other ventures in my business life, I struck out on my own to build my own publishing brand to publish what I wanted.

My wife and I had planned a vacation for our anniversary. We'd booked a trip to a wonderful resort on the Island of Antigua in the Caribbean. While lounging by the crystal-blue water of the pool, I finished the first draft of my second book, *A State of Treason*. Little did I know, the conspiracy theories that spilled from my imagination would come to life.

As my wife and I entered the customs area of Miami International Airport and we both swiped our passports, we were told to stand aside, that there was a "problem." The next thing we knew, three fully armed Homeland Security agents greeted us and asked us to follow them. We were rudely led into a large room that seemed to have hundreds of illegal aliens with sick, crying children. We were then told to wait on a bench. Neither of them would answer why or what type of problem existed with our passports.

My wife looked at me and asked what I did to get us back there. All I could think to answer was, "I joined the Tea Party, and I wrote a book...."

We had a two-hour window to catch a connecting flight to Houston, and I assured my wife that, surely, this would be straightened out in due time, and we would make our connecting flight so that she could spend time with our grandchild. It was a hollow promise—I had no idea why we were there or what they had in store for us. Finally, as we got perilously close to the time of our connecting flight, I went to the counter and demanded someone explain why we were being held. I was told to sit down and shut up or I would be handcuffed.

Another two hours passed, and no explanation. Finally, we were called to the counter, where we were unceremoniously split and taken into separate rooms. I told my wife, "Don't answer a damn question."

Once I got alone in the room with two agents, I proceeded to blast them, "endearing" them to us even further.

"What the hell are we doing back here? We are American citizens! I pay more in taxes every year than you two government employees make combined!"

They were equally as rude and proceeded to interrogate us separately, asking how much money we took to Antigua; how much we brought back; where we went while we were there; what business we conducted; if we visited any banks while on the island.

Of course, my answer to all their questions was, "It's none of your damn business." All along, I asked the agents to identify themselves, especially the man that came in to observe, who was in a suit and tie. I demanded to know why no agent at any time had his badge or nametag viewable. To this day, I couldn't tell you the name of anyone in that room.

Over the next few hours, they would send others in to ask the same questions, sometimes in a different way. I had no idea how my wife was holding up and demanded to see her. About an hour after that, we were finally back in one room together.

Again, we were interrogated — and my original hopes of pushing back defiantly into this intrusion of my civil rights turned into resignation, at which time I simply demanded an attorney. They continued to deny this request for several hours, leaving us alone in the room most of the time. I had to remind my wife not to say a thing, as cameras were everywhere.

Finally, after twelve exhausting hours, one lone agent came into the room and acted like he was going to be our friend. When we asked him as nicely as we could (given our abject anger) as to why we were being held without any charges or an attorney present, he simply flipped the computer monitor around and pointed to a "point" on the screen where they were instructed to "interview" us.

Thirty minutes later, they let us go. No explanation. No apology. No documents of any kind. As far as we know, there is zero record of us ever being held at U.S. Customs at Miami International Airport. Needless to say, I now had a surplus of material on conspiracy theories for my next political thriller, *Purge on the Potomac.*

For the next three years, we were audited again, for a total six straight years, for a grand total of nine audits in twelve years. During the last audit under the Obama administration in 2012, when we thought this was about over, we were issued a determination from the IRS for a year (2013) in which we were *never* audited! The same revenue agent that had audited us in 2012, determined that she would unilaterally deny all (yes, 100 percent of) expenses in business we had claimed, and she issued an amount due of several hundreds of thousands of dollars plus interest and penalties.

Between this and the Miami incident, it was apparent we were now playing in the big leagues, and our team wasn't up to the task. We engaged Mr. Bernhoft. Despite his wealth of experience and high-profile clients and cases, he had *never* seen the IRS issue an audit result without an *actual* audit! Although we never were penalized for any income we didn't report (we also report 100 percent), I figured it was a matter of time before the Obama administration trumped up some criminal charges against us, which is another reason Mr. Bernhoft was the right man for the job.

In trying to understand the reasons for, and correlation between, the repetitive audits, the disallowance of all legitimate business expenses, and the harassment in Miami, Mr. Bernhoft issued over seventy FOIA (Federal Freedom of Information Act) requests to the IRS, FBI, Homeland Security, and several other agencies to try to determine why the persecution persisted.

As of the writing of this book, we have the extreme pleasure to report that not one, not a single, solitary FOIA request from *any* agency—and particularly that of the IRS—has ever elicited a response.

We were able to raise enough hell inside the IRS to get our revenue agent changed and a more reasonable auditor put on the case; however, despite our struggles, I was still forced to go to tax court.

The way this system works, you have to pay the amount first then try to recover it. At one point, the legal fees, wasted time, stress, and other factors became larger than what was owed, and, on Mr. Bernhoft's advice, we settled, paying over $60,000, which was not legitimately owed, plus all my professional fees. It was less than one-eighth of what they originally disallowed, so there is *some* victory in that. I guess.

Fortunately for us, I had the financial means to fight them and a great tax attorney firm behind me. But, how many Americans get railroaded that may not have those means?

For now, the persecution has been paused since 2015, and I can't help but think it's no coincidence that the harassment stopped when President Trump took office. (Hear that? That is me knocking on wood as I type....)

During the height of this ordeal, in the middle of the gains made by the Tea Party politically, I kept telling my elected GOP representatives that my IRS targeting was not just about the 501-c organizations. I pleaded with them to investigate, that the administration had political enemies and somehow—because I participated in the political process, donated to a certain party or candidates, and was a successful business owner—I was targeted.

The truth of the matter is most politicians don't have the backbone and fortitude to stand up to the IRS. In fact, most have very little bravery when it comes to the IRS. To say that's disappointing would be an understatement. Sure, they can talk their fire and brimstone in a committee hearing or call for the end to the IRS. They can proclaim in political stump speeches that we could fill out our future tax returns on a postage stamp—but, at the end of the day, they know as well as anyone in America it's best not to poke the bear.

One of the benefits from the IRS audits is I've gained an understanding of how to make myself audit proof. I can't keep from getting an audit, but I have become a professional record keeper. As administrations change political hands, my advice would be to become audit proof like me. It doesn't mean you won't get audited—it only means that the better the record keeping, the less chance they have to disallow any legitimate expense or deduction.

You can never, ever convince me that the IRS is filled with good, reasonable, and honest human beings. My experiences with them, and especially revenue officers, are that they get their jobs because, like most government employees, they couldn't make it in the private sector. For instance, the last revenue officer who was in charge of auditing my multimillion-dollar business and personal tax returns didn't know the difference between a debit and a credit. My first auditor had very long fingernails on both of his pinky fingers. I am told people who grow those fingernails as such often use them for coke spoons, but, then, I really wouldn't know.

From that point forward, my tax professionals tried to keep me as far from IRS personnel as possible, and for good reason.

It takes a special kind of person to want to work for such a vile agency, to knowingly and willingly disrupt people's lives, and then lay their head on their pillow every night, sleeping comfortably.

Thanks to socialism and the progressive income tax, this is the type of America we find ourselves in—one that has very little in common with 1776.

For all IRS employees past, present, and future—may you rot in hell.

15

★

THE ROOT OF THE PROBLEM

"The income tax created more criminals than any other single act of government."

— Barry Goldwater (1909–1998)
Five-Term Senator from Arizona
Conservative Republican Presidential Candidate (1964)

W hy, if the socialistic progressive income tax is so great, is corruption in the IRS so rampant? Why, if Americans hate it so much, has there been no real effort to develop an alternative method for deriving the revenue the country needs to operate?

Until we foster the political will to alter this most basic and fundamental transgression of our God-given and Constitutional rights, nothing will happen. It's really quite simple if you boil the issue down to its most common denominators.

The fact is, most politicians and elected representatives don't want it to change. Additionally, it's arguable that most Americans have no stake in the game; therefore, they have no vested interested in seeing a sea-change in how we tax ourselves.

According to the Tax Policy Center, 76.4 million Americans (44.4 percent) do not pay *any* federal income tax. They state: "The top 0.1 percent of families pay the equivalent of 39.2 percent and the bottom 20 percent have negative tax rates. That is, they get more money back from the government in the form of refundable tax credits than they pay in taxes."[1]

I have always wondered how somebody could get "refunded" a tax credit that was never paid in throughout the previous tax year? That's not a "refund"; it's a gift!

If you're an American citizen who is essentially getting money for nothing, why would you want the system to change?

How popular would a politician be if he started telling his potential voters, "I'm sorry but you will now have to start paying into the system. After all, everyone has to pay their fair share."

The progressive socialists love to play on the "their fair share" argument as if the folks at the top of the income ladder aren't actually paying *more* than their fair share.

The mantra of the Democrats today is all about income equality, redistribution, and taxing the rich. The Republicans, dating back to the Teddy Roosevelt days, have never really figured out how to properly counter-message this socialist, populist, and Marxist ideology.

Politician after politician has caved over the years. The way Republicans fight this message is by tweaking the broken system with tax cuts, deductions, and special interest loopholes. They have learned how to divert the argument to marginal tax rates, income brackets, and quick fixes to play to their base. In the meantime, America sinks further away from our Forefathers' ideals.

And, of course, why do away with the sharpest tool in the shed? Both parties have figured out how to use the tax code to their advantage, punishing enemies and rewarding donors and cronies at will. Throughout history, the temptation to lift the skirt of private citizen's tax returns for political gain has always been much too inviting. Men who have monuments in Washington fashioned after their likenesses have used the IRS and the progressive income tax to defeat rivals and win elections. They've done this in back alleys, in the smoke-filled rooms of lowlife politicians and lifelong bureaucrats—and, yes, they've sent innocent people to jail in the process. Even the Oval Office—especially the Oval Office—uses this weapon, as the IRS sits under the Treasury Department, which is part of the Executive Branch of our government.

Status quo is the name of the game. The truth is, those in Washington, D.C. *benefit* from this Marxist system of taxation. The

Democrats win votes by promising to tax the rich (whatever "rich" means), by giving unearned tax refund checks, and by making somebody else pay the freight for running the federal government.

The Republicans promise tax cuts to marginal tax rates and corporate income tax rate reductions to curry donations and win elections. The GOP talks a big game about the "party" of small government and reduced taxes. Yet, they haven't delivered a smaller government once while they've had control of Congress and the White House since I've been born (1959). Instead, they continue to blow up the debt and pass every omnibus and continuing resolution bill that floats through Congress.

Then, of course, there is K Street in Washington, D.C., which is full of lobbyists. Their main target is the House Ways and Means Committee, where most spending and tax bills originate. It's arguably the most powerful committee on Capitol Hill.

Millions of dollars from special interest groups go into the members of that committee to influence spending and tax-writing policies. They all want their piece, their carve-out, their deduction, or their loophole. There's a reason the tax code is 77,000 pages long and it starts with this committee and the lobbyists.

And, finally, there is the tax industry. This industry is heavily invested in lobbying (as evidenced by the monies spent and political donations by H&R Block, Deloitte, PWC, KPMG, and others noted in Chapter 10). What in the world would these companies do to make a profit if they weren't doing tax returns as their basis for working with publicly-traded clients? What about all the CPAs in the country and smaller accounting firms?

Instead, maybe they could advise companies on how to increase profitability and streamline operations or consult on launching new businesses. This could be a good start.

There are some that would say getting your taxes in by April 15 every year is so ingrained in the American psyche, that it's as American as apple pie! What is more American than paying your taxes and getting a tax refund check?

If today's history books and our public schools were actually teaching the real history of 1776, our children would grow up cherishing the anti-tax fervor that led to the American Revolution and was instrumental in how the U.S. Constitution was formed.

As you can see, the challenge is formidable. The moneyed and politically-connected interests are deeply invested in keeping the progressive income tax as is — or, as we have been seeing lately from the Democrat Socialists, making it even more Marxist.

Our march to socialism started in earnest in 1913. Today, we are seeing the living results of the adoption of multiple Marxist platforms from *The Communist Manifesto*.

Can it be stopped? What type of herculean effort would it take to fix it permanently — or can it ever be fixed?

16

★

LIPSTICK ON A PIG

"Rather than passing a thousand pages of tax reform legislation and restarting the tax code manipulation process, we should change the paradigm. It is time to eliminate the IRS and repeal the 16th Amendment."

—Jim Bridgestone
Former U.S. Representative (Oklahoma)
Administrator of NASA

T he current tax reform recently delivered by the Trump Administration and Congress was ballyhooed to be the most significant tax reform in thirty years.

When studying the Tax Reform Act of 2017, which was passed into law, the social engineering aspects of it fly off the page.[1]

For example:

- Standard deductions were doubled (*populist move*).
- The child tax credit was doubled, of which $1,400 will be refundable (*despite not paying into federal income tax*).
- Deduction for home interest charges on residences with more than a $750,000 mortgage was eliminated (*a soak-the-rich proposition despite a $750,000 mortgage in many parts of the country being median housing value*).

- Deduction for state and local income, sales, and property taxes (SALT) were capped at $10,000 (another soak-the-rich feature).
- There are no casualty loss deductions unless you reside in a federally declared disaster area. (*If your house simply burns down, you're out of luck with any casualty loss deductions.*)
- Your heirs can keep the first $11.2 million you leave them before the government steals 40 percent of any inheritance over that amount.
- Small business pass-through deductions were increased.
- Corporate tax rates were reduced to 21 percent from 35 percent. (*They were extremely uncompetitive beforehand, and, now, this just puts the U.S. in the middle of the pack with competing countries.*)
- Pork-barrel carve-outs included tax breaks for citrus growers, film and television studios, alcohol and spirits, farmers, and opportunity zones in low-income areas.

The most significant reforms in thirty years?

By far, the feather in President Trump's cap regarding the 2017 Tax Act is the reduction of the corporate tax rate. Prior to this tax cut, the U.S. had the fourth highest corporate tax rate in the 202 jurisdictions surveyed by the Tax Foundation. The United States statutory corporate income tax rate is 15.92 percentage points higher than the worldwide average, and 9.5 percentage points higher than the worldwide average weighted by gross domestic product (GDP).[1]

When I see the talking heads spouting on television whether the tax plan was good or terrible, I am reminded of one of my favorite scenes in one of the all-time greatest movies ever made:

Scottish Noble: "Sir William, where are you going?"
Sir William Wallace: "We have beaten the English. But they will come back–because you won't stand together."
Scottish Noble: "But what will you do?"

Sir William Wallace: "I will invade England and defeat the English on their own ground."
Scottish Noble: "Ah, then? That's impossible."
Sir William Wallace: "Why? Why is that impossible? You're so concerned with squabbling over the scraps from Longshanks table that you've missed your God-given right to something better. There's a difference between us. You think the people of this country exist to provide you with possession. I think your possession exists to provide those people with freedom–and I go to make sure that they have it."

Braveheart©
Copyright by Icon Productions, The Ladd Company,
Paramount Pictures, & 20th Century Fox

Congressmen and congresswomen are *our* modern-day nobles. They think they exist to give Americans more free health care, tuition, welfare, food stamps, abortions, and income redistribution.

Like Scotsman William Wallace, I would argue their job is to give us more freedom.

Americans, unfortunately, have fallen into the trap of settling for the scraps from Congress's table. This tax act is not real reform. Real reform looks like something completely different (and I will describe it in the next chapter). It includes a mindset to change the entire structure of deriving revenue to fund those things — *and only those things*—that are enumerated in our glorious Constitution.

Americans have allowed themselves to be lulled to sleep over time. The average American now depends on their tax refund to catch up on credit card payments from Christmas or pay other bills. It is easy for them to forget it was their money in the first place and all they did was give Uncle Sam an interest-free loan for the year.

I even saw news reports how some taxpayers were unhappy with President Trump because their tax refund check was smaller than the year before. But, when pressed if their normal paychecks had increased due to fewer taxes being deducted each pay period, they had no idea how the increased take-home pay correlated into a smaller refund check. How easy is it for Congress to manipulate the masses if they can't even understand that tax cuts put more take-home pay in their checks and, for that tax year, they were actually better off than the year before?

No matter how many times Congress manipulates the tax code, they have been unable to substantially reduce its complexity over time. The hidden costs of the progressive income tax are enormous in compliance costs, non-compliance costs, and American competitiveness.

Change is difficult, and most people don't like change. Try to take away one of the sacred cows of the tax code (for instance, the home interest deduction) and see what type of reaction occurs. The possibility of eliminating one singular deduction emits a tremendous flurry of backlash from realtors, home builders, mortgage companies, the construction industry, the furniture industry, the home appliance industry, and many others—not to mention individual taxpayers who may not have another single itemized deduction on their tax return.

What politician can stand up to that type of pressure and tell all of those industries and taxpayers that it's better for the country? None can. They have never, and will never, be able to—unless, the political will and the associated political winds make a dramatic shift in direction.

There is no shared sacrifice in America. We have become a collection of opposed special interests fostered by a "what's in it for me?" mentality. The socialists from both parties have carefully groomed and nurtured this mindset for 106 years, and it's gotten us to where we are today. This mentality has been fertilized by the deplorable state of our educational system and run by liberal progressives who've fostered revisionist history and purposely bred the pride in American civics right out of two generations—and possibly forever.

We demand answers to the wrong questions. We seek absolution in a progressive income tax system where there is none. They project so-called social justice through our mandatory participation.

We live under a constant but generally unspoken threat.

Americans are having entirely the wrong conversations about taxes. Arguing over marginal tax rates and itemized deduction allowances is exactly where Karl Marx wanted us.

And here we are.

17

---★---

THE FLAT TAX AND THE FAIRTAX

"In the 1880s, people all over the world looked to America for inspiration. Its very existence was proof that it was possible to have a relatively free and peaceful country. No income tax, no foreign wars, no welfare state, no intrusions on civil liberties."

—Harry Browne (1933–2006)
1996 Libertarian Party Presidential Candidate & Author

The original income tax, levied by Congress after the Sixteenth Amendment was ratified, was a tax on one percent of the net personal incomes above $3,000 ($76,962 in today's dollars) with a six percent surtax on incomes above $500,000 ($12.83 million in today's dollars). With those types of numbers, the income tax touched very few Americans. This was, in essence, a flat tax, as the surtax only reached a few of the very wealthiest in America.

Just a few short years later, in 1918, Congress boosted the top marginal tax rate to 77 percent.

The Sixteenth Amendment did not prescribe a tax rate; it arguably only amended the Constitution to allow a direct tax on individuals. Congress sets the tax rates—and they've never gotten it right.

The two problems with a flat tax should be obvious to every liberty-minded American. First, as long as Congress is involved, it will never stay "flat." And, even if there were such a thing as a flat income tax (much like a unicorn, it's never actually been seen), it still has one major flaw. It doesn't get rid of the IRS!

That dark angel would still be looming on our doorsteps, ready to invade our privacy and rob us of our Bill of Rights at a moment's notice. It would also not remove the temptation by politicians to encourage audits of political enemies. The Gestapo-state would still exist. And, the progressive socialists would only see it as an opportunity, manipulating it for their many special interests.

No matter how grand flat tax proponents make that type of system sound (it would be better than what we have if it were truly flat), it would still tax labor and productivity; it would still have huge compliance costs; and, it would still leave vulnerable the opportunity for just one carve-out to turn into thousands of complex tax code, which brings us right back to where we are today. Besides, what progressive politician from either party could resist sticking their hand in the cookie jar?

I've been a proponent of a consumption tax, somewhat in fashion with the FairTax. Although this has been one of the more legitimate alternatives presented for an income tax replacement, the movement has been met with serious resistance. That is always how you know something could legitimately work—when socialists complain how "regressive" it is.

Consumption or sales tax proponents run into trouble when discussions move to what rate of sales tax it would take to fund the government. Of course, that is the wrong argument completely.

When consumption or national sales proponents float the notion of 23–25 percent sales tax, it meets immediate resistance. Again, just like you saw with the citizens who complained their refund check was smaller despite netting more take-home pay for the year, like with civics, Americans are generally not good at math, either.

I've seen national sales tax proponents explain ad infinitum to confused faces. "Since you're no longer getting federal income tax withholding, your net take home is immediately larger, and the sales tax is not the burden it would be if you were paying the sales tax on top of your federal withholding."

The national sales tax idea is much more aligned with how our Founders intended for government to be funded: through excise taxes and import duties.

The sales tax proponents have some challenges to overcome, besides the inherent self-interests of all the special interest groups, and lobbyists and socialists who love our current inefficient and unfair tax system. If a national sales tax is implemented, yet the Sixteenth Amendment isn't repealed, we run the very real risk of eventually having *both*! When have you ever seen the federal government (or any government entity of any kind) roll back revenues they're already receiving? Never.

So, unless there is some way to lock up the progressive income tax and throw away the key forever, we always run the risk of ending up with both—and, in fact, I would bet that could be likely. That makes the task of implementing a national sales tax so much more complicated and riskier.

Secondly, the proposals for a national sales tax have a rate too high for the average American to get behind. When we start adding 23–25 percent to the cost of everyday goods, products, and services it can appear daunting.

Why is this percentage the range of most national sales tax proposals? Because the proponents are modeling it on a *revenue-neutral* model. This means it takes this much sales tax to produce the same amount of revenue from the current income tax to fund government. If government were cut down to its proper size and scope per the Constitution, this sales tax number would likely be in the low, single digits.

Socialists focus heavily on the regressive nature of the national sales tax. Notice how the income tax nomenclature is "progressive" and the other solutions are "regressive"? This implies that socialists consider the application of any regressive tax plan would mean taking a higher percentage of overall income from lower-income Americans. That certainly doesn't portend well for their social justice and income redistribution schemes. It's impossible for them to buy votes this way, so it is a nonstarter.

National sales tax proponents, recognizing this argument, have proposed "prebates" wherein low-income Americans would get a check every year for a certain amount based on their income to offset the percentage of income they pay in national sales tax for necessities. Some of these plans begin as high as $7,000 per year per family!

Please tell me where I can find this form of welfare in the U.S. Constitution.

This is where I get off the train. This is no better example than the earned income tax credits that people who pay no federal taxes receive now. It's another form of welfare. Why would we pay this *upfront*?

Instead, why not have a foolproof identification card that allows a low-income person to be exempt from sales tax at the point of purchase? Like a food stamp card, the card-carrying purchaser would have to be present (using available facial or retinal scanning technology); that way, only the purchaser could be exempt from sales tax on necessities.

Sending a check to recipients in advance of them "doing something" to qualify for it is not the American way and we need to erase this notion from our consciousness.

No more IRS. That alone makes the national sales tax idea the best one to me. How would the government collect the money without the IRS? This is the simplest part of the entire equation. The method already exists.

When a retail purchase of any kind is transacted, the retailer (or point of sale) collects the sales tax and remits it to the state comptroller or facsimile thereof. They would also collect the national sales tax and remit that to the federal treasury, with the states receiving a stipend portion of the sales tax to cover their cost of collection.

The IRS could be disbanded and spread to the wind—forever.

Studies have shown the effect of this type of revenue source conversion—the results could be historically impactful to the economy. Few consider how much federal taxes and compliance costs play into the price of goods and services. Additionally, the extra cash in consumers' pockets could jolt the economy, creating a lasting impact.[1]

Imagine being able to control how much you pay in taxes simply by controlling how much you spend—and what you spend it on? Politicians and government bureaucrats would be loathe for Americans to see what the cost of their government really is when they are right there at the cash register!

I'm sure some things would be exempt from the national sales tax—and that would be a healthy debate. Even the Founders had to determine what products to apply excise taxes and import duties to.

Any move to a consumption tax will be fought by the *Deep State* and the socialists to their last breath because it removes their power. It is hard to see how any consumption or national sales tax can gain the political power necessary to supplant the monster that feeds the *Deep State*. Unless there are accompanying deep cuts in spending, the sales tax rate is likely too high to be sold to the public on a revenue-neutral basis.

18

★

UNDERSTANDING THE ENEMY

"The state is no longer satisfied merely with raising an adequate source of revenue, but now considers it a duty to interfere with the rights of private property in or to bring about a more equitable distribution of wealth."

—Edwin R.A. Sigelman (1861–1939)
Columbia University Economist
Leading Proponent of Progressive Income Tax

It is important to fully understand that the progressive socialists are not simply content with the level of progressive income taxation we currently have. They want more—a lot more—of what you and I earn.

The following Socialist Party platform is very clear on how far they want to go:

Steeply graduated income tax, capital gains, & luxury tax
- We call for a steeply graduated income tax and a steeply graduated estate tax, and a maximum income of no more than ten times the minimum. We oppose regressive taxes such as payroll tax, sales tax, and property taxes.
- We call for the restoration of the capital gains tax and luxury tax on a progressive, graduated scale.
- We call for compensation to communities—and compensation, re-training, and other support services

for workers—affected by plant and military base
closings as stop-gap measures until we reach our goal
of creating a socialist society totally separate from the
global capitalist economy.
- We support tax benefits for renters equal to those for
homeowners.
- We call for the elimination of subsidies and tax breaks
that benefit corporations and all other forms of
corporate welfare.

Steeply graduated income tax and estate tax
- We call for a steeply graduated income tax and
graduated estate tax, plus the restoration of capital
gains and luxury taxes on the same basis. We also
oppose regressive taxes such as payroll tax, sales tax
and property taxes.

The socialists would prefer to have property taxes on an "ability
to pay" just as income tax is, meaning a progressively higher rate
based on income or wealth.

Limit maximum income to ten times minimum income
- minimum wage of $15 per hour, and cost-of-living
increases
- support livable guaranteed annual income
- call for a steeply graduated income tax and estate tax,
and a maximum income of no more than 10 times
minimum.

A maximum income of ten times the minimum wage? If
minimum wage were $15 per hour, then under the socialists, any
income above $312,000 would be illegal ($15/hour x 10 x 4
hours/week x 52 weeks/year). Luxury taxes have been proven to
destroy entire industries. A guaranteed annual income? We are
already starting to see some municipalities and states where this is
being proposed.

More progressive taxation, especially on runaway industry

192

- We call for full disclosure of corporate plans to close and relocate plants, a punitive tax on runaway industry, and compensation for the workers and communities affected by plant closings.
- We support a single-payer National Health Program, publicly funded through progressive taxation, and controlled by democratically elected local boards.[1]

A single-payer health care monstrosity is one of the socialists' most important rallying cries; after all, they believe access to health care is a human right. What they don't say is it's a human right that you and I shouldn't be made to pay for someone else's access to health care.

Almost the entire platform of the socialists involves an increase in our taxes. It's important to fully understand the impact of the values of the Socialist Party according to Ballotpedia:

- *Economics:* Only a global transformation from capitalism to democratic socialism will provide the conditions for international peace, justice, and economic cooperation based on the large-scale transfer of resources and technology from the developed to the developing countries.
- *Imperialism:* We stand in total opposition to U.S. imperialism and the current "war on terror" which is just another subterfuge for U.S. imperialism.
- *Labor:* The Socialist Party stands for the right of all workers to organize, for worker control of industry through the democratic organization of the workplace, for the social ownership of the means of production and distribution, and for international solidarity among working people based on common opposition to global capitalism and imperialism.
- *Racism:* The Socialist Party recognizes the intimate link between racism and capitalism and demands the elimination of all forms of discrimination in housing, jobs, education, health care, etc.

- *Gender equality:* The Socialist Party is a socialist feminist organization that recognizes that a struggle against habitual male dominance and patriarchy must go hand in hand with any struggle against capitalism. Therefore, we pledge our opposition to all forms of sexism, and demand equality in all aspects of life.
- *Education*: The Socialist Party recognizes the right of students of all ages to a free, quality education in a safe and supportive environment, and of all school employees to good wages, benefits, and working conditions.
- *Healthcare*: The Socialist Party stands for a socialized health care system based on universal coverage, salaried doctors and health care workers, and revenues derived from a steeply graduated income tax.
- *Immigration*: The Socialist Party works to build a world in which everyone will be able to freely move across borders, to visit and to live wherever they choose. We recognize the central role global capitalism plays in forcing the immigration of people from the less developed to the more industrialized countries, often leading to further economic and social injustice.
- *Environment:* We call for public ownership and democratic control of all our natural resources in order to conserve resources, preserve our wilderness areas, and restore environmental quality.
- *Energy:* The Socialist Party stands for municipal ownership and control of energy plants, in a non-profit and decentralized, but coordinated, system that ensures the most careful use of natural resources.[1]

As radical as these socialist positions would seem today, we are seeing the manifestation of decades of liberal indoctrination in our education system. These positions have become mainstream enough that Democrats are openly espousing Marxist theories on a wide range of political and social issues.

Every item in this partial list of Socialist Party platform ideals involves the ability to shift the huge costs of social programs onto the backs of the producers. This can only lead to more taxes and a heavier burden for those paying the majority of the freight in the current progressive income tax system.

19

★

CONSERVATIVE ACTION PLAN

"The spirit of resistance to government is so valuable on certain occasions that I wish it to be always kept alive."

—Thomas Jefferson (1743–1826)
3rd U.S. President
Founding Father
Author of the Declaration of Independence

D on't ever, ever accept it.
Not anymore.
Not ever.

A socialistic progressive income tax system is un-American. We can no longer tolerate the mere acceptance of the status quo on this subject from *any* political party.

Make no mistake about it. The GOP has its share of blame in allowing the Sixteenth Amendment to get ratified in the first place. You can rank Teddy Roosevelt with some of the worst presidents in American history on his promotion of a Marxist ideal alone.

Blasphemy for Republicans?

The truth hurts.

From time to time, we hear Republicans who are running for office talk about a national sales tax, a flat tax on a postcard, or doing away with the IRS. Mostly, it's a gimmick to gin up support of the base.

The progressive income tax has become so ingrained into the American psyche that only a political re-awakening will ultimately end this stain on American history. Who will be the statesman or stateswoman to lead us out of this darkness?

In 2010, we saw a political movement called the Tea Party become a big enough force to hand President Obama a significant defeat in the mid-term elections. It was a political sea change.

I grew up with the Berlin Wall being impregnable, a sign of the strength of the Communist Soviet Union. One man's dream was able to topple a wall that most thought would stand forever. Ronald Reagan spoke his vision into reality, a political tidal wave that swept America to victory in the Cold War.

Assuming that "all politics are local," this is where we need to start. Below, is a section from the GOP Platform on Taxes. It's time we had Republicans trumpet this stance with an action-plan to phase out the progressive income tax and the IRS:

Our Tax Principles (GOP)

To ensure that past abuses will not be repeated, we assert these fundamental principles. We oppose retroactive taxation. We condemn attempts by activist judges at any level of government to seize the power of the purse from the people's elected representatives by ordering higher taxes.

We oppose tax policies that deliberately divide Americans or promote class warfare. Because of the vital role of religious organizations, charities, and fraternal benevolent societies in fostering generosity and patriotism, they should not be subject to taxation and donations to them should remain deductible. To guard against hypertaxation of the American people in any restructuring of the federal tax system, any value added tax or national sales tax must be tied to the simultaneous repeal of the Sixteenth Amendment, which established the federal income tax.[1]

This is a good start and something to build on — but where is the detailed plan?

Where is it specifically stated that the GOP is against a progressive income tax?

198

When in control of both houses of Congress and the White House, the GOP has had opportunities aplenty to fix Obamacare and immigration. They've failed because of their inability to build a plan and then get consensus.

The grassroots activists need to begin to press local and state party leadership to start adopting a more definitive plan and an achievable timetable. Let me stress: promoting a revenue-neutral plan, wherein government spending is not reduced substantially, will kill any new initiatives to rid ourselves of Karl Marx's ideology.

The civic illiteracy of Americans is abysmal. Conservatives should seriously consider supplementing the public education system with their own at-home version of American history and civics. American children should be taught to cherish the proud anti-tax history of the American Revolution.

Parents should actually read their children's history and government textbooks and be involved in choosing curricula. The outgrowth of democratic socialism for the last two generations is due to the proliferation of intentional ignorance in American history, civics, and the Constitution. Millennials' attraction to a socialist platform has been fostered by Democrats and their sense of a growing plutocracy.

Capitalism isn't a bad word, but most millennials don't know how to participate. They feel the system is rigged. They have been taught that they can't get ahead to realize the American Dream because wealth is a zero-sum game: if you have it, they can't get it; ergo, the producers owe it to them.

They must be won over by free enterprise.

America needs a new commitment to *free enterprise* and to promote the renewed growth of its economic engine: small business. Free enterprise should be taught at the earliest ages in public schools, and more universities should have degree paths in entrepreneurship. The entrepreneur should be elevated to national hero status, not necessarily celebrating massive monetary success but the achievement of independence and freedom.

Imagine a life without the IRS standing in the shadows behind you. Imagine a life where you keep 100 percent of what you make and, whatever you make, *that's* your take-home pay. Imagine a life where April 15 is just another day. You're not scrambling to get your taxes done or waiting on the government to send you a refund check (i.e., give you back your own money).

Regarding the Marxist ideology of the leftists, the Republican Party should publicly disavow the progressive income tax with stronger conviction than it ever has. With the socialists now appearing to be driving the direction of the Democrats, the timing is perfect to draw the absolute distinctions between capitalism and socialism by yanking out the teeth of the most important weapon the progressive socialists have at their disposal: the graduated income tax.

The Bill of Rights was meant to apply to *every* American under *every* circumstance. These God-given and natural rights disappear at the door of the IRS or in United States tax court.

It's been proven that the very nature of the IRS and the progressive income tax facilitates corruption in the agency itself—and at the highest levels of government. It's time to take this massive tool out of the playbook of those who use it for political ends.

An American system of taxation and revenue should be entirely neutral, transparent to the taxpayer, completely blind to politics, and incorruptible. It should be pro-growth for the economy and have no winners or losers. A new system of taxation should follow the original Constitution and not have direct taxes on the individual, requiring each citizen to be directly involved with his or her federal government.

It's time to start asking every political candidate—at every level of government, including school boards, local, state, and federal—for a debate on this topic. Where do you stand on the progressive income tax? The best remedy to this insidious disease is to shed sunlight on its origin, its purpose, and its ties to Marxism.

It's time to hold so-called conservative leaders responsible to deliver on their promises, to revitalize the vision of our Founders, to finally shed the yoke of this oppressive form of taxation on America.

Now that you have learned how we got to this place in history, what will *you* do to *today*, to advance this cause of *Liberty*?

REFERENCES

Chapter 1: Have We Lost Our Sense of Liberty?

1. "Employment Projections Home Page." U.S. Bureau of Labor Statistics. Accessed December 2018.
    https://www.bls.gov/emp/tables/employment-by-major-industry-sector.htm.
2. "Whiskey Rebellion." Wikipedia. December 28, 2018. Accessed March 4, 2019.
    https://en.wikipedia.org/wiki/Whiskey_Rebellion.
3. Editorial Board. 2018. *The Wall Street Journal*. October 4. www.WSJ.com.
4. Office of Management & Budget. 2018. WhiteHouse.gov.
5. Marx, Karl and Friedrich Engels. 2017. Chapter 2. *The Communist Manifesto*. New York: International Publishers. First published in 1848 by the Communist League.
6. "BLS Data Inflation Calculator." U.S. Bureau of Labor Statistics. Accessed December 2018.
    https://www.bls.gov/data/inflation_calculator.htm.
7. "U.S. Inflation Calculator." U.S. Bureau of Labor Statistics. Accessed December 2018.
    https://www.usinflationcalculator.com.
8. Joseph, Richard J. 2004. *The Origin of the American Income Tax: The Revenue Act of 1894 and Its Aftermath*. Syracuse, New York: Syracuse University Press.
9. Jeffrey, Terence P. "Feds Collect Record Individual Income Taxes in FY 2018; Still Run $779B Deficit." CNS News. October 16, 2018. Accessed December 8, 2018.
    https://www.cnsnews.com/news/article/terence-p-jeffrey/feds-collect-record-individual-income-taxes-fy-2018.

Chapter 2: Progressivism & the Roots of American Class Warfare

1. "Second Industrial Revolution." Wikipedia. September 29, 2018. Accessed December 8, 2018.
    https://en.wikipedia.org/wiki/Second_Industrial_Revolution.
2. Blackburn, Robin. 2012. "Lincoln and Marx." *Jacobin Magazine*. August 28, 2012.
    https://jacobinmag.com/2012/08/lincoln-and-marx.
3. DiLorenzo, Thomas J. 2003. *The Real Lincoln*. New York, New York: Three Rivers Press. 134–142, 254–256, 252–253.

4. Brians, Paul. "Misconceptions, Confusions, and Conflicts Concerning Socialism, Communism, and Capitalism." Washington State University. Accessed December 2018.
        https://brians.wsu.edu/2017/04/14/7273/.
5. Waltman, Jerold L. 1985. *The Political Origins of the U.S. Income Tax.* Jackson, Mississippi: University Press of Mississippi.
6. "Knowlton v. Moore." FindLaw. Accessed December 29, 2018.
        https://caselaw.findlaw.com/us-supreme-court/178/41.html.
7. Ratner, Sidney. 1942. *American Taxation: Its History as a Social Force in Democracy.* New York: W.W. Norton & Company, Inc. 17, 243–247.

Chapter 3: Teddy Roosevelt: The Progressive's Trojan Horse

1. Hatfield, Mark O. "U.S. Senate Art & History: Vice Presidents of the United States." U.S. Government Printing Office. Accessed December 9, 2018.
        https://www.senate.gov/artandhistory/history/resources/pdf/garrett_hobart.pdf.
2. Ratner, Sidney. 1942. *American Taxation: Its History as a Social Force in Democracy.* New York: W.W. Norton & Company, Inc. 252–255.
3. Davis, Shelley L. 1993. *IRS Historical Fact Book: A Chronology, 1646–1992.* Washington, D.C.: Andesite Press. 79–80.
4. Folsom, Burton W. 2010. "Teddy Roosevelt and the Progressive Vision of History." Foundation for Economic Education (FEE). September 22. Accessed December 25, 2018.
        https://fee.org/articles/teddy-roosevelt-and-the-progressive-vision-of-history/.
5. Tax History Project—The Seven Years' War to the American Revolution. Accessed December 25, 2018.
        http://www.taxhistory.org/www/website.nsf/Web/THM1901?OpenDocument.
6. Pestritto, Ronald J. and William J. Atto, eds. "New Nationalism Speech." In *American Progressivism: A Reader*, 211-223. Lanham, Maryland: Lexington Books, 2008. Accessed December 25, 2018.
        http://teachingamericanhistory.org/library/document/new-nationalism-speech/.
7. "Whiskey Rebellion." Wikipedia. December 28, 2018. Accessed March 4, 2019.
        https://en.wikipedia.org/wiki/Whiskey_Rebellion.
8. Hoyt, Alia. "How Socialism Works." HowStuffWorks. March 12, 2008. Accessed December 28, 2018.
        https://money.howstuffworks.com/socialism3.htm.

Chapter 4: Constitutional Taxes

1. "Articles of Confederation." Wikipedia. Accessed December 29, 2018. https://en.wikipedia.org/wiki/Articles_of_Confederation.
2. "The Constitution of the United States: A Transcription." National Archives and Records Administration. Accessed December 29, 2018. https://www.archives.gov/founding-docs/constitution-transcript.
3. "Anti-Federalism." Wikipedia. Accessed December 29, 2018. https://en.wikipedia.org/wiki/Anti-Federalism.
4. "Anti-Federalist Papers: Brutus #6." Constitution Society: Everything Needed to Decide Constitutional Issues. Accessed December 29, 2018. http://www.constitution.org/afp/brutus06.htm.
5. DiLorenzo, Thomas J. 2003. *The Real Lincoln.* New York, New York: Three Rivers Press.
6. Davis, Shelley L. 1993. *IRS Historical Fact Book: A Chronology, 1646–1992.* Washington, D.C.: Andesite Press. 31.
7. *New York Times.* "Views from the Capital." *Work of the Extra Session of Congress.* November 2, 1862. 5–8.
8. "Springer v. United States, 102 U.S. 586 (1880)." Justia Law. Accessed January 6, 2019. https://supreme.justia.com/cases/federal/us/102/586/.
9. "U.S. Inflation Calculator." U.S. Bureau of Labor Statistics. Accessed December 2018. https://www.usinflationcalculator.com.
10. "McKinley Tariff." Wikipedia. November 8, 2018. Accessed December 31, 2018. https://en.wikipedia.org/wiki/McKinley_Tariff.
11. *The Globe.* "A Week's Income." February 10, 1894.
12. "Pollock v. Farmers' Loan & Trust Co., 157 U.S. 429 (1895)." Justia Law. Accessed December 31, 2018. https://supreme.justia.com/cases/federal/us/157/429/.
13. "Nicol v. Ames." FindLaw. Accessed December 29, 2018. https://caselaw.findlaw.com/us-supreme-court/173/509.html.
14. "Knowlton v. Moore." FindLaw. Accessed December 29, 2018. https://caselaw.findlaw.com/us-supreme-court/178/41.html.

Chapter 5: The GOP's Grand Mistake

1. Davis, Shelley L. 1993. *IRS Historical Fact Book: A Chronology, 1646–1992.* Washington, D.C.: Andesite Press. 80–82.
2. Pestritto, Ronald J. and William J. Atto, eds. "New Nationalism Speech." In *American Progressivism: A Reader,* 211-223. Lanham, Maryland: Lexington Books, 2008. Accessed December 25, 2018. http://teachingamericanhistory.org/library/document/new-nationalism-speech/.

Chapter 6: "Pay as You Go"—A Direct Assault on Liberty

1. Power. "Vivien Kellems: Tax Resister, Feminist, and Industrialist." History News Network. June 07, 2006. Accessed January 12, 2019.
   http://historynewsnetwork.org/blog/26413.
2. "Vivien Kellems Takes On the IRS." Connecticut History. April 7, 2017. Accessed January 2019.
   https://connecticuthistory.org/vivien-kellems-takes-on-the-irs/.
3. "Vivien Kellems." Wikipedia. November 09, 2018. Accessed January 12, 2019.
   https://en.wikipedia.org/wiki/Vivien_Kellems.
4. Kellems, Vivien. *Toil, Taxes and Trouble*. New York, New York: E.P. Dutton & Co. Inc., 1952. 17–31.
5. Davis, Shelley L. 1993. *IRS Historical Fact Book: A Chronology, 1646–1992*. Washington, D.C.: Andesite Press. 128.
6. Ruml, Beardsley. 1946. "Taxes for Revenue Are Obsolete." *American Bar Association Journal* (January 1946 Edtion): 36.
7. Roosevelt, Franklin D. 1942. *President Franklin D. Roosevelt Message to Congress*. Washington, D.C.: White House.
8. Amy Fontinelle. 2010. *Investopedia: Tax Withholding: Good for Government, Bad for Taxpayers*. Investopedia. February 22. Accessed January 19, 2019.
   https://www.investopedia.com/articles/tax/10/tax-withholding-benefits-criticisms.asp.
9. Marx, Karl and Friedrich Engels. 2017. *The Communist Manifesto*. New York: International Publishers. First published in 1848 by the Communist League. 30.

Chapter 7: Whose Money Is It? The Morality of the Income Tax

1. Secretary, White House Press. 2012. "Remarks by the President at a Campaign Event in Roanoke, Virginia." Washington D.C.: White House.
2. Warren, Elizabeth. 2018. Accessed February 2, 2019.
   https://elizabethwarren.com/tax-returns/.
3. Rubin, Jenniffer. 2012. "Obama is losing his message like nobody's business." *The Washington Post*, July 24: unknown.
4. McCann, Steve. 2011. *American Thinker*. American Thinker. March 9. Accessed January 2019.
   https://www.americanthinker.com/articles/2011/03/confiscate_americans_wealth_to.html.
5. Elise Labott, Nicole Gaouette and Levin Liptak. 2016. *U.S. Sent Plane with $400 Million in Cash to Iran*. CNN Politics. August 4. Accessed March 1, 2019.
   https://www.cnn.com/2016/08/03/politics/us-sends-plane-iran-400-million-cash/index.html.
6. 2019. *Foreign Assistance.Gov*. USA.GOV. Accessed March 1, 2019.

https://www.foreignassistance.gov/explore.

7. U.S. Census Bureau. 2015. *U.S. Census Bureau.* May 28. Accessed January 19, 2019.
https://www.census.gov/newsroom/press-releases/2015/cb15-97.html.

8. U.S. Census Bureau. 2015. *United States Census Bureau Fast Facts.* Accessed January 19, 2019.
https://www.census.gov/history/www/through_the_decades/fast_facts/1880_fast_facts.html.

9. Early, John F. 2018. "Reassing the Facts about Inequality, Poverty and Redistribution." *Cato Institute Policy Analysis* 839: 24.

10. Tanner, Michael. 2016. "Five Myths about Income Inequality in America." *Cato Institute Policy Analysis* (September 7, 2016): 29.

11. Bedard, Paul. 2018. *Washington Examiner.* "Census Confirms: 63 Percent of 'Non-Citizens' on Welfare, 4.6 Million Households." Accessed March 14, 2019.
https://www.washingtonexaminer.com/washington-secrets/census-confirms-63-percent-of-non-citizens-on-welfare-4-6-million-households?fbclid=IwAR2z8fHSA_PoiOOEGm-O2TvNDDQIWFUnVMtD_6hORLtgwMkCuK81zBbm3mk.

12. Rahn, Richard W. 2010. "Morality and the IRS." *Washington Times,* April 6.

13. Smith, Adam. 1776. *An Inquiry Into the Nature and Causes of the Wealth of Nations.* London: W. Strahan and T. Cadell.

14. Jacobson, Louis. 2015. *PolitiFact.* Poynter Institute. November 10. Accessed January 21, 2019.
https://www.politifact.com/truth-o-meter/statements/2015/nov/10/ted-cruz/ted-cruz-says-us-tax-code-has-more-words-bible/.

15. Feldman, Jason J. Fichtner & Jacob M. 2013. "The Hidden Costs of Tax Compliance." *Mercatus Research Center George Mason University,* May 20: 21.

16. 2019. *The Truth About Frivolous Arguments.* Internal Revenue Service. Accessed March 2, 2019.
https://www.irs.gov/privacy-disclosure/the-truth-about-frivolous-tax-arguments-section-i-d-to-e#_Toc350157901.

17. 2019. *U.S. Debt Clock.* USDebtClock.org. Accessed March 2, 2019.
http://www.usdebtclock.org/#.

18. David Cay Johnston. 2006. *IRS to Cut Tax Auditors.* New York Times. July 23. Accessed March 3, 2019.
https://www.nytimes.com/2006/07/23/business/23tax.html.

19. 2013. *Socialism and the Estate Tax: Legalized Theft.* The Reeves Law Firm. February 26. Accessed March 3, 2019.
https://reeveslawfirm.wordpress.com/2013/02/26/socialism-and-the-estate-tax-legalized-theft/.

Chapter 8: Patriotism & Paying Taxes

1. Sickle, Eugene Van. n.d. *The War of 1812 Financing*. BandyHeritageCenter.org. Accessed January 26, 2019. http://www.bandyheritagecenter.org/Content/Uploads/Bandy%20Herit age%20Center/files/1812/Financing%20the%20War%20of%201812.pdf.
2. Davis, Shelley L. 1993. *IRS Historical Fact Book: A Chronology, 1646–1992*. Washington, D.C.: Andesite Press. 92, 132.
3. Williamson, Vanessa S. 2017. *Read My Lips: Why Americans Are Proud to Pay Taxes*. Princeton, NJ: Princeton University Press. 3, 8–10, 36.
4. Lavoie, Richard. 2011. "Patriotism and Taxation: The Tax Compliance Implications of the Tea Party Movement." *Loyola of Los Angeles Law Review* (September 1, 2011): 86.
5. United States Treasury Department. 2019. *Treasury Direct*. January 4. Accessed February 2, 2019. https://www.treasurydirect.gov/govt/reports/pd/gift/gift.htm.
6. 2018. "The World's Highest Paid Celebrities." *Forbes Magazine*. Accessed February 2, 2019. https://www.forbes.com/celebrities/list/#tab:overall.
7. Afreen Hidayat. 2018. "Startup Stories." Accessed February 2, 2019. https://www.startupstories.in/stories/top-5-highest-paid-ceos-in-2018.
8. 2019. *Net Worth Bro*. Accessed February 2, 2019. https://networthbro.com/hillary-clinton-net-worth/.
9. Hillary Hoffower. 2019. *Business Insider*. January 19. Accessed February 2, 2019. https://www.businessinsider.com/barack-obama-michelle-obama-net-worth-2018-7.
10. 2018. *FinApp.Co*. Accessed February 2, 2019. https://finapp.co.in/nicolas-cage-net-worth/.
11. Brooke Rogers. 2015. *National Review*. July 1. Accessed February 2019. https://www.nationalreview.com/2015/07/nancy-pelosi-wealth-liberal-hypocrisy/.
12. Christopher Cadelago. 2016. *Sacramento Bee*. October 17. Accessed February 2, 2019. https://www.sacbee.com/news/politics-government/capitol-alert/article108767562.html.
13. Alexandra Hutzler. 2018. *Newsweek*. June 23. Accessed February 2, 2019. https://www.newsweek.com/bernie-sanders-makes-one-million-dollars-second-straight-year-book-deals-992845.
14. Warren, Elizabeth. 2018. Accessed February 2, 2019. https://elizabethwarren.com/tax-returns/.

Chapter 9: The Benevolent State via the Income Tax

1. Kim Dixon. 2014. *Politico*. December 9. Accessed February 2, 2019.

https://www.politico.com/story/2014/12/child-tax-credit-fraud-113425.

2. Robert Rector & Jamie Hall. 2016. *The Heritage Foundation.* November 16. Accessed February 2, 2019.
    https://www.heritage.org/welfare/report/reforming-the-earned-income-tax-credit-and-additional-child-tax-credit-end-waste.

3. Bob Segall. 2012. "Tax Loophole Investigation." Channel 13 WTHR. May 8. Accessed December 2018.
    https://www.wthr.com/article/tax-loophole-investigation.

4. General, Treasury Inspector. 2011. *United States Treasury.* July 7. Accessed February 2, 2019.
    https://www.treasury.gov/tigta/auditreports/2011reports/201141061fr.pdf.

5. David North. 2017. "Congress Takes a Step Against Paying Illegal Aliens to Stay in the U.S." The Center for Immigration Studies. December 7. Accessed March 11, 2019.
    https://cis.org/North/Congress-Takes-Step-Against-Paying-Illegal-Aliens-Stay-US.

Chapter 10: Compliance Costs—Paying for Your Loss of Freedoms

1. 2018. "Statistics Times." May 6. Accessed February 4, 2019.
    http://statisticstimes.com/economy/countries-by-projected-gdp.php.

2. Scott A. Hodge. 2016. "Tax Foundation." June. Accessed February 4, 2019.
    https://files.taxfoundation.org/legacy/docs/TaxFoundation_FF512.pdf.

3. Feldman, Jason J. Fichtner & Jacob M. 2013. "The Hidden Costs of Tax Compliance." *Mercatus Research Center George Mason University,* May 20: 21.

4. Demian Brady. 2018. *Policy Paper: Tax Complexity 2018.* Washington, D.C.: National Taxpayers Union Foundation.

5. Alex Tabarrok. 2011. "The 57,000 Page Tax Return." *Marginal Revolution.* November 22. Accessed February 7, 2019.
    https://marginalrevolution.com/marginalrevolution/2011/11/the-57000-page-tax-return.html.

6. 2018. *Open Secrets.* Open Secrets.org. Accessed February 11, 2019.
    https://www.opensecrets.org/orgs/recips.php?id=D000022016&cycle=2018&state=&party=&chamber=&sort=A&page=1.

Chapter 11: The Progressive's Secret Weapon: Fear

1. Internal Revenue Service. 2018. "Form 1040 U.S. Individual Income Tax Return." Washington, D.C: U.S. Department of the Treasury.

2. *Tax Debt Help.* Tax Debt Help. Accessed February 11, 2019.
    https://www.taxdebthelp.com/tax-problems/tax-audit/irs-audit-statistics.

3. *TRAC IRS.* Syracuse University. Accessed February 11, 2019.
    https://trac.syr.edu/tracirs/.

4. Block Advisors. 2017. Washington Business Journal. March 29. Accessed February 11, 2019.
   https://www.taxdebthelp.com/tax-problems/tax-audit/irs-audit-statistics.

5. "United States v. Sullivan, 274 U.S. 259 (1927)." Justia Law. Accessed January 6, 2019.
   https://supreme.justia.com/cases/federal/us/274/259/.

6. Adam Andrzejewski & Thomas W. Smith. 2016. *The Militarization of America: Non-Military Federal Agencies Purchase of Guns, Ammo, and Military-Style Equipment.* Burr Ridge, IL: Open the Books.

7. Caron, Paul. 2016. "Why Does The IRS Need So Many Guns?" *TaxProfBlog.* June 17. Accessed February 2, 2019.
   https://taxprof.typepad.com/taxprof_blog/2016/06/why-does-the-irs-need-so-many-guns.html.

8. Someka. n.d. "Fortune Global 500 List." *Someka Excel Solutions.* Accessed February 2011, 2019.
   https://www.someka.net/excel-template/fortune-global-500-list/.

9. Governing. n.d. *Governing The States and Localities.* Governing.com. Accessed February 11, 2019.
   http://www.governing.com/gov-data/federal-employees-workforce-numbers-by-state.html.

10. Department of the Treasury. 2018. "Congressional Justification for Appropriations 2018." Accessed February 11, 2019.
    https://www.treasury.gov/about/budget-performance/CJ18/05.%20%20IRS%20-%20FY%202018%20CJ.pdf.

11. Kohler, Mark J. 2016. "The Top Ten Ways to Avoid an IRS or State Audit." *Entrepreneur.* February 19. Accessed February 12, 2019.
    https://www.entrepreneur.com/article/270948.

12. "[Study] 1 in 4 Americans Afraid They Will be Audited by the IRS." December 3, 2018. Lexington Law. Accessed February 11, 2019.
    https://www.lexingtonlaw.com/blog/news/irs-audit-preparedness.html.

13. 2017. *Internal Revenue Service Data Book, 2017.* Washington, D.C.: Internal Revenue Service. 67.
    https://www.irs.gov/pub/irs-soi/17databk.pdf.

14. FederalPay.org. 2019. *Pay Rates for Internal Revenue Agents.* FederalPay.org. Accessed February 11, 2019.
    https://www.federalpay.org/employees/occupations/internal-revenue-agent/2016.

15. Megan McArdle. 2016. "Commentary: Why We Fear the IRS." *Chicago Tribune,* January 5.

16. Joe Weisenthal. 2010. "The Insane Manifesto of Austin Texas Crash Pilot Joseph Andrew Stack.*" Business Insider.* Accessed February 17, 2019.
    https://www.businessinsider.com/joseph-andrew-stacks-insane-manifesto-2010-2.

17. Andrea Ball. 2010. *Dallas News.* The Dallas Morning News. March. Accessed February 17, 2019.

https://www.dallasnews.com/news/texas/2010/03/03/Hatred-toward-IRS-nothing-new-676.

18. Treasury Inspector General for Tax Administration. 2013. *Potentially Dangerous Taxpayer and Caution Upon Contact Cases Are Adequately Controlled, but Improvements in Training and Outreach Are Needed.* Washington, D.C.: Department of the Treasury.

19. 2019. "The Result of IRS Unpaid Back Taxes—Horror Stories." *Highland Tax Group.* January 4. Accessed February 17, 2019.
    https://highlandtaxresolution.com/penalty-reduction/the-result-of-unpaid-irs-back-taxes-horror-stories.

Chapter 12: The Horror Stories

1. Ross Kenneth. 2012. *Tax Audit Horror Stories: When the IRS Attacks.* AOL.com. February 28. Accessed February 17, 2019.
    https://www.aol.com/2012/02/28/tax-audit-horror-stories-irs/.

2. n.d. *Painful Tax Return, Audit Experiences.* eFile.com. Accessed February 17, 2019.
    https://www.efile.com/painful-taxpayer-irs-audit-experiences-tax-stories/.

3. 2019. *Tax Horrors That Will Give You Nightmares.* IRS.com. Accessed February 17, 2019.
    https://www.irs.com/articles/tax-horror-stories-will-give-you-nightmares.

4. Lisa Ferguson. n.d. "Lessons Learned: How One Entrepreneur Lost His Business Afer an IRS Tax Audit." *BPlans.* Accessed February 17, 2019.
    https://articles.bplans.com/lessons-learned-how-one-entrepreneur-lost-his-business-after-an-irs-tax-audit/.

5. n.d. *Trader Status.* Trader Status. Accessed February 17, 2019.
    https://traderstatus.com/tax-planning/audited/horror-stories/.

6. n.d. "IRS Horror Stories." *Stop IRS Debt.* Accessed February 17, 2019.
    https://www.stopirsdebt.com/irs-horror-stories/.

7. Nick Wing. 2016. "IRS Returns Bakery's Money After 3 Years. Now It Wants to Put the Owners in Prison." Huffington Post. May 25. Accessed February 23, 2019.
    https://www.huffingtonpost.com/entry/irs-structuring-civil-asset-forfeiture_us_573b908de4b0aee7b8e83ae3.

8. Kate Rogers. 2016. "Small Businesses Still Fighting for Cash Seized by IRS." CNBC. February 17. Accessed February 23, 2019.
    https://www.cnbc.com/2016/02/17/small-businesses-still-fighting-for-cash-seized-by-irs.html.

9. Shaila Dewan. 2015. "Rules Change on IRS Seizures, Too Late for Some." *New York Times.* April 30. Accessed February 23, 2019.
    https://www.nytimes.com/2015/05/01/us/politics/rules-change-on-irs-seizures-too-late-for-some.html.

10. Shaila Dewan. 2014. "Law Lets IRS Seize Accounts on Suspicion, No Crime Required." *New York Times*. October 25. Accessed February 23, 2019.

   https://www.nytimes.com/2014/10/26/us/law-lets-irs-seize-accounts-on-suspicion-no-crime-required.html?module=inline.

11. 2014. Statement of Richard Weber, Chief of IRS Criminal Investigation. *New York Times*. October 25. Accessed February 23, 2019.

   https://www.nytimes.com/2014/10/26/us/statement-of-richard-weber-chief-of-irs-criminal-investigation.html?_r=0&module=inline.

12. Jason Pye. 2018. "A Last Shot at Reining in IRS Abuse of Asset Forfeiture in the 115th Congress." *Freedom Works*. December 4. Accessed February 23, 2019.

   http://www.freedomworks.org/content/last-shot-reining-irs-abuse-asset-forfeiture-115th-congress.

13. Tessa Berenson. 2017. "Jeff Sessions Wants Cops to Seize More Money from Suspected Criminals." *Time*. July 19. Accessed February 24, 2019.

14. 2017. *IRS.Gov*. IRS. September 29. Accessed February 23, 2019.

   https://www.irs.gov/compliance/criminal-investigation/statistical-data-for-three-fiscal-years-criminal-investigation-ci.

Chapter 13: Punish Thine Enemies

1. Jr., Burton W. Folsom. 2008. *New Deal or Raw Deal? How FDR's Economic Legacy has Damaged America*. New York, NY: Simon & Schuster.

2. 2013. *American Communists*. Real Clear Politics. May 15. Accessed February 24, 2019.

   https://www.realclearpolitics.com/lists/irsscandal/american_communists.html.

3. David Burnham. 1989. "Misuse of the IRS: The Abuse of Power." *New York Times Magazine*.

4. 1974. *Watergate Info*. Watergate.Info. July 27. Accessed February 24, 2019.

5. Paula Corbin Jones. 2013. *History of IRS Abuse*. Real Clear Politics. May 15. Accessed February 24, 2019.

   https://www.realclearpolitics.com/lists/irsscandal/paula_corbin_jones.html?state=stop.

6. House Committee on Oversight & Government Reform. 2014. *The Internal Revenue Service's Targeting of Conservative Tax-Exempt Applicants: Report of Findings for the 113th Congress*. Washington, D.C.: U.S. House of Representatives.

7. Kelly Phillips Erb. 2016. *IRS Targeting Scandal: Citizens United, Lois Lerner and the $20M Tax Saga That Won't Go Away*. Forbes. June 24. Accessed February 24, 2019.

   https://www.forbes.com/sites/kellyphillipserb/2016/06/24/irs-targeting-scandal-citizens-united-lois-lerner-and-the-20m-tax-saga-that-wont-go-away/#76883e35bcd1.

Chapter 15: The Root of the Problem

1. Quentin Fottrell. 2019. "More than 44% of Americans Pay No Federal Income Tax." *MarketWatch*. February 26. Accessed February 26, 2019.
    https://www.marketwatch.com/story/81-million-americans-wont-pay-any-federal-income-taxes-this-year-heres-why-2018-04-16.

Chapter 16: Lipstick on a Pig

1. Kari Johnson. 2017. *Corporate Income Tax Rates Around the World 2017*. Tax Foundation. September 7. Accessed February 26, 2019.
    https://taxfoundation.org/corporate-income-tax-rates-around-the-world-2017/.

Chapter 17: The Flat Tax and the FairTax

1. 2017. *The Economy*. FAIRtax.org. October 16. Accessed March 23, 2019.
    https://fairtax.org/research-library/the-economy

Chapter 18: Understanding the Enemy

1. 2019. *Socialist Party on Tax Reform*. OnTheIssues.org. Accessed March 3, 2019.
    https://www.ontheissues.org/celeb/Socialist_Party_Tax_Reform.htm.

Chapter 19: Conservative Action Plan

1. 2019. *GOP Platform*. Republican Party. Accessed March 3, 2019.
    https://gop.com/platform/.

INDEX

$500 million, 61
1787, 30
1825, 30
1861, 31, 32, 191
1862, 31, 205
1890, 16, 35, 37
1894, 35, 203, 205
1895, 35, 58, 205
1898, 17
1899, 36
1900, 36
1900s, 11, 22, 37, 87
1904, 20, 25
1909, 39, 175
1911, 39
1912, 25, 26
1913, 1, 79
1927, 42, 211
1935, 44, 156
1937, 44
1942, 48, 204, 206
1948, 42
1965, 62
1970s, 63, 65
1990, 100, 105
1991, 66, 103
2002, 66, 74, 168
2006, 41, 134, 168, 185, 206, 208
2009, 168
2015, 61, 93, 135, 138, 148, 172, 207,
    208, 209, 213
2016, 11, 97, 99, 100, 101, 112, 113,
    115, 137, 152, 155, 207, 209, 210,
    211, 212, 213, 214
2017 Tax Act, 180
2018, 35, 61, 90, 102, 105, 106, 112,
    203, 204, 205, 206, 207, 209, 210,
    211, 213, 214
3.5 years, 25
39.6 percent, 64
50 percent, 64
70 percent tax rate, 56
Abraham Lincoln, 11, 31
Adam Smith, 71
advocate, 23, 89
Affordable Care Act, 103

African, 61
Air Force, 112
Al Capone, 111
Alabama, 39
Albert Gallatin, 80
Alexander Hamilton, 28, 30, 166
Alexandria Ocasio-Cortez, 56
America, 4, 7, 9, 1, 11, 15, 31, 39, 45,
    56, 58, 59, 61, 62, 66, 68, 73, 74, 78,
    79, 80, 81, 85, 86, 88, 90, 99, 100,
    104, 153, 165, 173, 176, 185, 198,
    207, 211, 213
American, 11, 13, 16, 17, 21, 22, 23,
    26, 27, 31, 34, 41, 44, 45, 55, 57, 59,
    61, 66, 76, 78, 79, 80, 81, 82, 84, 85,
    86, 87, 88, 89, 101, 104, 106, 107,
    112, 114, 116, 119, 141, 147, 149,
    158, 163, 167, 170, 176, 177, 181,
    182, 185, 187, 188, 197, 198, 200,
    203, 204, 206, 207, 214
American Bar Association, 44, 206
American Revolution, 79, 84, 88, 204
American Taxation, 17, 204
American Thinker, 55, 207
Andrew Clyde, 148
Andrew Jackson, 30
Andrew Mellon, 157
Anti-Federalists, 29, 30
anti-tax, 79, 85, 86, 87, 88, 89
apathetic, 48
apportioned, 28, 31, 33, 35, 58, 68
April 14, 1906, 22
April 15, 177, 200
April 27, 1942, 45
Army, 27, 112, 145
Articles of Impeachment, 158
audited, 69, 106, 109, 110, 125, 127,
    129, 158, 159, 168, 173, 213
Bandy Heritage Center, 80
Barack Hussein Obama, 53
Barack Obama, 90
Barry Goldwater, 175
Ben Franklin, 71
Benghazi, 165
Berlin Wall, 198
Bernie Sanders, 90

Bessemer, 13
Bill of Rights, 30, 110, 121, 145, 186,
    200
Black Panthers, 158
Blaine Luetkemeyer, 105
Bob Segall's "Tax Loophole", 93
Boston Tea Party, 87
British, 59, 79
Brown & Root, Inc., 157
Brutus VI, 29
Bureau of Internal Revenue, 156
bureaucracy, 83, 104, 118
Burton W. Folsom, 21, 213
Business Master File, 103
CAFRA, 148
Capitalism, 14, 204
Capitol Hill, 126, 177
Carole Hinders, 134, 143
Catholic University, 73
Cato Institute, 207
CAU, 117, 118
caution upon contact, 117
Center for Immigration, 97, 210
Chairman, 148
Channel 13, 93, 210
Chicago Tribune, 115, 212
China, 61
Christian, 59, 158
Chrysler Building, 42
citizenry, 45, 48, 69, 81, 153
Citizens United v. FEC, 162
Civil Asset Forfeiture Reform Act,
    147, 148
Claire McCaskill, 105
Clara Barton, 41
class warfare, 38, 39, 54, 56, 81, 198
Clay Sanford, 117
Clinton administration, 159
Clyde Armory, 148
CNBC, 140, 213
Cold War, 198
colonists, 27, 48, 69, 79
Columbia, 42, 191
Commodore Vanderbilt, 31
common Defense, 71
Communist Party USA, 158
compliance, 69, 74, 84, 85, 86, 89, 99,
    100, 101, 132, 182, 186, 213
Congressman Vallandigham, 12
Connecticut, 40, 41, 42, 126, 130, 131,
    132, 134, 206
Constitutional Convention, 28, 59
constitutionalist, 42

consumption tax, 57
Continental Army, 27
corrupt, 58, 61
corruption, 62, 70, 161, 162, 165, 200
county tax collector, 71
Criminal Investigation, 118, 144, 145,
    152, 213
cronyism, 63
Crown, 48
Dallas Morning News, 116, 212
Darrell Issa, 162
David Smith, 144
David Vocatura, 130, 131, 132, 135
Dean Heller, 105
Dean Patterson, 140
death tax, 78
December 7, 1907, 23
Defense Tax, 82
Democrat, 25, 26, 157
Democratic-Republican, 30
Department of Health, 101
Department of Justice, 135, 138, 140
Departments of Defense and
    Agriculture, 112
Deputy Chief Counsel, 126
Donald Rumsfeld, 129
Doug Shulman, 162
Douglas Shulman, 159
Dr. Martin Luther King, Jr., 75
Drug Enforcement Agency, 149
Due Process Act, 137, 138, 147
Eastern District of North Carolina,
    142
Edgar, 42, 157
Edwin R.A. Sigelman, 191
Eleanor Roosevelt, 41
Elizabeth Warren, 90, 105
Elliott Roosevelt, 156
Emanuel Cleaver, 105
employers, 41, 44, 48, 102
Enforcement, 113, 121, 137, 147, 149
English king, 27
entrepreneurs, 22
Equal Rights Amendment, 27, 41
Eric Holder, 165
Erik Hurst, 62
Estate Tax, 208
Eugene V. Debs, 26
evasion, 22, 87
excess, 45, 47
excise taxes, 12, 31, 34, 56, 80, 82, 187,
    189
Fair Act, 149

fair share, 48, 56, 89, 176
Fast and Furious, 165
Father Charles Coughlin, 157
Father of Communism, 99
FDR, 24, 45, 47, 156, 157, 165, 213
federal, 17, 22, 27, 28, 29, 31, 33, 34,
     38, 42, 48, 49, 51, 56, 59, 71, 74, 77,
     80, 81, 83, 89, 100, 103, 104, 106,
     111, 112, 117, 118, 119, 123, 130,
     133, 134, 135, 137, 143, 144, 145,
     147, 148, 149, 156, 157, 158, 166,
     179, 186, 187, 198, 205, 211, 214
federal government, 17, 27, 28, 29, 31,
     38, 48, 51, 59, 71, 78, 80, 89, 100,
     103, 106, 112, 118, 119, 130, 135,
     143, 156, 166, 187
Federal Reserve Bank of Boston, 62
Federalist No. 51, 21, 29
Feminist, Industrialist, 41
Fifth Amendment, 164
First Amendment right to Freedom of
     Religion, 59
flat tax, 57, 81, 82, 185, 197
Flint v. Stone Tracey Company, 39
Foreign Account Tax Compliance
     Act, 103
foreign aid, 61, 75
Fortune 500, 106, 112
Foundation for Economic Education,
     21, 204
Founding Fathers, 1, 29, 71
Four-Minute Men, 81
Frank Chodorov, 1
Frank Murphy, 157
Franklin D. Roosevelt, 24, 45, 82, 156,
     206
Frédéric Bastiat, 37, 65, 72
Frederick Engels, 14
Freedom of Information Act Request,
     103
Freedom of Religion, 59
GAO, 103
Garrett Hobart, 20
Gary Becker, 65
GDP (Gross Domestic Product), 99
General Electric, 104
George Clooney, 90
George Holding, 142
George Mason University, 73, 208,
     210
George W. Bush, 159
George Washington Bridge, 42

George Washington University's
     Columbian College of Arts &
     Sciences, 41
GOP, 11, 25, 26, 37, 38, 39, 40, 173,
     198, 206, 215
graduated income tax, 22, 23
graft, 62, 75
grave national danger, 45
Greenpeace, 159
gross receipts taxes, 12
H&R Block, 102, 105, 106, 177
H.R.3860, 106
H.R.5444, 106
H.R.5445, 106
Happiness, 58
harbor terrorists, 61
Harry Browne, 185
Hellen Mardaga, 73
Henry Hyde, 148
Heritage Foundation, 159, 209
Hillary Clinton, 65, 90
home mortgage interest deduction,
     107
House Committee on Ways and
     Means, 138
House of Representatives, 21, 47, 162,
     214
House Ways, 106, 140, 177
House Ways and Means Committee,
     106, 177
Hughey P. Long, 156
Human Services, 71, 101
IBISWorld, 101
ignorance, 70
illegal aliens, 75, 92, 93, 97
immigration, 92, 194
income inequality, 31, 53, 62, 63, 64,
     68
incompetence, 32, 62, 70, 109, 118
incumbent, 26, 47
Indiana on WTHR, 93
Individual Master File, 103
individual tax return audits, 110
Indonesia, 75
industrialists, 14, 37
industrialization, 11, 14
inequality, 62, 63, 64, 65, 66, 67, 68
inheritance taxes, 12, 31
Institute for Justice, 131, 132, 134,
     135, 136, 138, 139, 140, 143, 144,
     146, 149
interest-free loan, 181
Internal Revenue Service (IRS), 148

Internal Revenue Service Data Book, 211
investment income, 77
Investopedia, 206
Iran, 59, 207
IRS Commissioner, 138, 155, 164
IRS Inspector, 97
J. Edgar Hoover, 157
James Madison, 21, 28, 30
Jean-Jacques Rosseau, 14
Jennifer Rubin, 55
JFK, 158
Jim Bridgestone, 179
Jim Sensenbrenner, 137, 147
Joan Barthel, 126
Joe Stack, 115
Joe the Plumber, 53
John Birch Society, 157
John Jay, 28
John Koskinen, 138, 142, 155
Joint Economic Committee, 66
Jordan, 127
Jordan Markuson, 127
Joseph Sobran, 79
Judicial Watch, 159
July 1, 1862, 12
July 1906, 38
July 2012, 53
July 4, 1906, 20
June 1907, 38
Justice White, 17
K Street, 177
Kamala Harris, 90, 105
Karl Marx, 11, 14, 24, 156
Katy Perry, 90
Kellems Cable Grips in Manhattan, 42
Kevin Brady, 105, 106
Kevin McCarthy, 105
Khalid "Ken" Quran, 140
King George III, 48, 79
Knowlton v. Moore, 36, 204, 206
Ku Klux Klan, 158
Larry Salzman, 146
late 1800s, 11, 13, 16, 36
lawsuits, 39
legal costs, 146
Lenin, 153
Leslie Moonves, 90
levied, 45, 158, 185
Lexington Law, 211
Liberty, 4, 11, 47, 53, 58, 69, 75, 149, 200, 203, 206
licenses taxes, 12

Lois Lerner, 162, 164, 214
Lucy Burns, 41
Ludwig Von Mises, 91
luxury tax, 66, 191
Lyndon McLellan, 135, 141
Madison, Wisconsin, 55
Main Street U.S.A., 30
mandatory, 44, 45
marauding bands, 54
Mark Aguiar, 62
Mark J. Kohler, 113
Marxist, 45, 55, 57, 73, 74, 176, 194
Mayor Frank Hague, 157
Megan McArdle, 115, 212
Melissa Kearney, 64
Melody Thornton, 118
Mercatus Center, 73
Mexico, 92
Michael Moore, 55
Mike Lee, 143
military defense, 57
monarchy, 27
moral, 30, 37, 41, 68, 69, 72, 75, 87
Mr. Pollock, 35
Mr. W.B. Astor, 31
Murray Newton Rothbard, 41
NAACP, 157, 159
Nancy Pelosi, 90
Nation of Islam, 158
national coal strike, 21
National Council of Churches, 157
National Defense Authorization Act, 119
National Legislature, 32
National Rifle Association, 159
national sales tax, 187, 198
National Taxpayer Advocate, 74, 104
National Taxpayers Union, 101, 210
National Taxpayers Union Foundation, 101, 210
Navy, 112
NBC's Meet the Press, 42
NDAA, 119
New Jersey governor, 39
New Nationalism, 22, 24, 38, 204, 206
New York, 31, 32, 35, 42, 126, 134, 137, 143, 144, 145, 203, 204, 205, 206, 207, 208, 213, 214
New York subway system, 42
New York Times, 31, 32, 134, 143, 144, 145, 205, 208, 213, 214
Nicol v. Ames, 206
Nicolas Cage, 90

Nina Olson, 104
Nobel Economics Prize, 65
Nobel Peace Prize, 19
non-citizens, 208
nondiscriminatory, 71
Nucky Hague, 157
Nuremberg, 70
Obama administration, 59, 110, 163, 165, 172
Obamacare, 97, 163, 169
Open Secrets, 105, 210
Open the Books, 211
Oval Office, 166, 176
PACs (political action committees), 105
Painful Tax Return Audit Experiences, 122
Paperwork Reduction Act, 100
parliament, 28, 79
Patrick Henry, 29, 119
Patriotic Remittance Tax, 85
Paul Hatz, 121
Paula Jones, 159
Pay as You Go, 11, 206
Payne-Aldrich Tariff Act, 39
PDT, 116, 117, 118, 119
Pearl Harbor, 81, 82
per capita, 58
Peter Carr, 144
Peter Orszag, 64
Peter S. Jongbloed, 132
Piketty, 64, 65
Planned Parenthood, 59, 75
Politburo, 81
Pollock v. Farmers' Loan & Trust Company, 35
potentially dangerous taxpayer, 116, 117
Pravda, 81
pre-paying, 51
President Grover Cleveland, 35
President Roosevelt, 44
President Trump, 1, 165, 173, 180, 181
presidents, 19
privilege, 24, 39, 48
Progressive Era, 21, 26, 37, 45, 53, 61, 62, 76
progressive income tax, 21, 81, 88, 105, 106, 176, 182
progressives, 17, 20, 38, 44, 46, 48, 51, 56, 57, 62, 81, 84, 85, 88, 89, 90, 91, 92, 119

Progressivism, 11, 203, 204, 206
property taxes, 71, 180, 191, 192
protective legislation, 41
punishing the rich, 63, 65
railroad trusts, 20
Rand Paul, 143, 149
Randy and Karen Sowers, 139
Randy Nowak, 117
ratification, 28, 39
redistribution, 57, 64, 66, 71, 105, 107, 156, 176, 181, 187
reducing poverty, 63, 68
reelection, 156, 165
regressive, 57, 186, 187, 191, 192
religious beliefs, 59, 76
repeal, 179, 198
Republican Party, 20, 30, 215
return-free, 102
revenue, 18, 28, 31, 32, 34, 35, 39, 44, 58, 61, 64, 72, 73, 76, 80, 81, 83, 101, 106, 112, 113, 115, 127, 128, 156, 157, 175, 191, 212
Revolutionary War, 27
Rhode Island, 40, 130
Richard Nixon, 158
Richard W. Rahn, 69
Richard Weber, 144, 213
Rights of Life, 58
robber barons, 15, 16, 22, 37
Robert Everett Johnson, 132, 139, 143
Robert G. Bernhoft, 11, 168
Robert Half, 121
Robert Jackson, 157
Ronald Reagan, 198
Rosa Parks, 41
S.3246, 106
S.3278, 106
S.912, 106
Samuel Adams, 119
San Juan Hill, 23
Satya Nadella, 90
Schedule C expenses, 114, 168
Scottish Enlightenment, 71
Second Industrial Revolution, 11, 203
seize, 54, 110, 130, 133, 141, 146, 147, 148, 198, 213
self-dealing, 70
Shay's Rebellion, 86
Shelly L. Davis, 80
Sherman Anti-Trust Act of 1890, 16
Sherrod Brown, 105
Sixteenth Amendment, 26, 36, 39, 40, 42, 159, 185, 187, 198

slavery, 61
social change, 81
social feminists, 41
social justice, 20, 57, 76, 91, 105, 156, 187
Social Security Act, 44
Socialist Party, 26, 191, 193, 194, 195, 215
Son of Thunder, 119
South Mountain Creamery, 139
Southern Christian Leadership Conference, 158
Soviet Union, 198
Spanish-American War, 80
Springer v. United States, 34, 205
Stalin, 153
stamp taxes, 12
state, 17, 27, 28, 29, 34, 39, 45, 55, 56, 58, 61, 63, 71, 74, 76, 87, 110, 123, 124, 133, 134, 180, 185, 186, 191, 210, 211, 214
state capitals, 55
State of Virginia, 39
Steve McCann, 55
Steve West, 142
Steven L. Kessler, 137
successful, 22, 37, 56, 111, 173
Sudan, 61, 75
Sugar Act, 79
Sundar Pichai, 90
Supreme Court, 23, 31, 34, 35, 39, 76, 157, 162
Susan B. Anthony, 41
Sydney Ratner, 17
Syracuse University, 110, 203, 211
take-home pay, 48, 181, 199
tax, 11, 12, 17, 20, 22, 23, 27, 28, 31, 32, 33, 34, 35, 36, 37, 38, 39, 40, 41, 42, 44, 45, 46, 48, 51, 56, 57, 58, 59, 61, 62, 63, 64, 66, 69, 70, 71, 72, 73, 74, 75, 76, 77, 78, 79, 80, 81, 82, 83, 84, 85, 86, 87, 88, 89, 90, 91, 92, 93, 97, 99, 100, 101, 102, 103, 104, 105, 106, 107, 109, 110, 112, 113, 114, 115, 117, 118, 119, 121, 122, 124, 125, 126, 127, 128, 129, 130, 132, 143, 145, 152, 153, 156, 157, 159, 162, 163, 164, 165, 166, 168, 169, 172, 173, 175, 176, 177, 179, 180, 181, 182, 185, 186, 187, 188, 189, 191, 192, 193, 194, 195, 197, 198, 200, 206, 207, 208, 209, 210, 211, 212, 213, 214

tax code, 51, 63, 69, 70, 72, 73, 74, 81, 99, 103, 104, 105, 106, 107, 109, 110, 113, 115, 117, 121, 145, 157, 165, 176, 177, 179, 182, 186
tax collectors, 41, 71
tax liability, 51, 58, 75, 128
tax on tea, 27
Tax Resister, 41, 206
Teddy Roosevelt, 11, 19, 25, 26, 37, 45, 81, 176, 204
Thaddeus Stevens, 12
The Articles of Confederation, 27
The Communist Manifesto, 51, 203, 207
The Deterring Undue Enforcement by Protecting Rights of Citizens from Excessive Searches and Seizures Act, 147
The Federalist Papers, 28
the Gilded Age, 11
The Globe, 35, 205
the New Deal, 157
The Stamp Act, 79
The Tax Foundation, 99
The Wealth of Nations, 71
Thomas Jefferson, 30, 119, 197
TIGTA, 149
Tim and Tracey Kerin, 125
TIN (tax identification number), 97
Tom Pendergast, 157
Townsend Act, 79
TRAC program, 110
Treasury Department, 90, 121, 140, 156, 162, 176, 209
Treasury Inspector General, 104, 117, 149, 212
Treasury Inspector General for Tax Administration, 104, 117, 149
Trump, 9, 78, 134, 165, 166, 179
U.S. history, 19
U.S. House of Representatives Committee on Oversight and Government Reform, 162
U.S. Senator Elizabeth Warren, 54
unconstitutional, 11, 22, 23, 35, 36, 45, 58, 80, 131
unconstitutional limits, 45
undemocratic, 58
Under penalties of perjury, 109
unionism, 55
United States, 4, 9, 1, 11, 19, 33, 58, 61, 63, 67, 73, 74, 75, 76, 84, 85, 86, 87, 88, 92, 97, 98, 126, 142, 158,

180, 200, 204, 205, 207, 209, 210, 211
United States attorney, 142
United States v. Lee, 76
United States v. Sullivan, 211
University of Chicago, 62
University of Oregon, 42
unpatriotic, 42, 80, 87
upper-income, 57, 62
Utah, 40, 143, 167
Utah Phillips, 167
Veterans Affairs, 112
Victory, 48
Virginia, 39, 40, 53, 128, 144, 145, 207
Vivien Kellems, 27, 41, 45, 206
Vladimir Lenin, 99
Vocatura's, 130, 131, 138
wage earners, 143
Wall Street, 203
Wall Street Journal, 203
War of 1812, 80, 208
War on Poverty, 67
War Revenue Act, 17, 31
Washington, 14, 41, 42, 55, 69, 73, 111, 144, 156, 162, 176, 177, 204, 205, 206, 207, 208, 210, 211, 212, 214
Washington Examiner, 207
Washington Post, 55, 207

Washington State University, 14, 204
Washington Times, 69, 208
Washington, D.C, 156, 177, 204, 205, 206, 208, 210, 211, 212, 214
Watergate Scandal, 158
wealthy, 17, 37, 56, 64, 66, 67, 157
Weekly Standard, 104
What Is Seen and What Is Not Seen, 65
Whiskey Rebellion, 86, 203, 205
White House, 21, 45, 76, 160, 163, 164, 165, 206, 207
William Gale, 64
William H. Taft, 25
William Jennings Bryan, 25
William Randolph Hearst, 157
Wilson-Gorman Tariff, 35
withholding, 41, 44, 48, 51, 59, 110, 158, 186, 206
Women's Suffrage, 42
Women's Suffrage and Equal Rights, 42
Woodrow Wilson, 26
Works Progress Administration, 157
World War I, 81
World War II, 45, 46, 80, 81
WPA, 157
Wyoming, 40
Yemen, 61, 75

THE DEATH OF LIBERTY©